Kicking the Habit

ELEANOR STEWART

LION

Published by Lion Books
an imprint of
Lion Hudson plc
Wilkinson House, Jordan Hill Road,
Oxford OX2 8DR, England
www.lionhudson.com/lion

ISBN 978 0 7459 5611 4
e-ISBN 978 0 7459 5770 8

First edition 2013

Acknowledgments
Scripture quotations are taken from The Jerusalem
Bible, published and copyright 1966, 1967 and 1968
by Darton, Longman & Todd Ltd and Doubleday
and Co. Inc, and used by permission of the
publishers.

A catalogue record for this book is available from
the British Library

Printed and bound in the UK, May 2013, LH26

Contents

Acknowledgments

To my husband, John, who has encouraged me from the beginning.

To my children, Esme and Paul, who have never allowed me to take myself too seriously.

To Philip Clark, for his wonderfully generous, unstinting support, advice, and guidance over so many years.

Also to Ali Hull of Lion Hudson, whose recommendations I sometimes followed reluctantly but which proved to be correct.

Note to the reader: For those who are unfamiliar with the terminology of convent life, you will find a helpful glossary at the end of the book.

PART 1

Entry

CHAPTER 1

An Ordinary Girl

"Would you like a drink?" Susan's question to me, in the roomy Caravelle aircraft that brought us to France on a sunny September day in 1961, was posed in the lofty tones of the seasoned air traveller.

"A drink?" I said uncertainly. I was beginning to feel a bit unsure of myself, despite my self-conscious sophistication. I had never been on an aeroplane before. Did one pay for drinks? What sort of drinks did one have? In the end, she took pity on me, although I had been so cocky up until then she could have been forgiven for taking a slightly malicious satisfaction in putting me on the spot.

"I'm going to have a sherry," she said at last. Gratefully, I accepted one too.

I was nowhere near as confident as I looked; uncertainty about the drink had rattled me and I began unexpectedly to have an overwhelming feeling of general apprehension. *What the devil am I doing?* I thought. *And where the devil am I going?* It's one thing to think about becoming a nun in the abstract, to stun your friends with your announcement, to decide to take the plunge when you are sitting at home with the reassuring support and pride of your mother, and quite another to find yourself literally flying toward it. My hands felt clammy. I hadn't even looked up my final destination on a map, for heaven's sake; I only knew that the Mother House was in a small town in the heart of rural France. What had seemed a lovely adventure when I first set off was becoming frightening. I looked at my companion out of the corner of my eye, wondering if I wanted a drink at all.

Following Susan, I stumbled out of the Arrivals hall. A young, slim, and very pretty nun was waiting for us. With admirable efficiency, she collected our suitcases and shepherded us outside. She was supremely aloof, and ignored the low catcalls she got from the assembled taxi drivers. Summoning one with a raised hand, which I noticed had beautifully cared-for fingernails, she bundled us into the cab.

"Isn't she elegant!" I whispered, looking at her black habit, snow-white headband, and neat but floating veil. My companion was silent. There is something very unsettling about a comment being ignored. I barely knew Susan, who was going to enter the convent with me; I did hope she was not going to remain quite so distant.

Paris was shimmeringly hot and unbelievably exotic. The traffic, the buildings, the crowd, the noise and chatter crowded in on me. It was a barrage of sound, and all of it incomprehensible. I was a small-town girl and the panic attack on the plane was forgotten. *I might never be here again. I mustn't miss anything,* I thought. I offered up a quick prayer: "Thank you, dear Lord, for helping me to choose this French congregation." I remembered some of the grim English ones I had met on exploratory visits to other convents. Certainly my proud sophistication began to slip a bit; I was as excited as a schoolgirl, which was what I was! Susan and the pretty nun exchanged a few words as we drove through the streets, the former translating as we went along.

"We're going to have lunch in the Sisters' convent in Rue de Roule, and then perhaps go out to see a bit of the city," said Susan. "Our train isn't until this evening." She gave me a thin smile, which I returned, determined not to be put off by her coolness. It was understandable; we had no common ground apart from entering the same religious congregation as postulants at the same time. If I was horribly brash and affected, then she, older than me, had all the reserve that foreigners associate with the English. She was a highly qualified music teacher and I a barely educated teenager. Propinquity made us friends in the end; our Englishness allowed us to present a united front against some of the more arcane customs that we would meet during our noviciate.

The convent was a tenement flat in a narrow street behind the recently demolished market "Les Halles", leaving, I was told, "the biggest hole in Europe". The sisters ran an inexpensive canteen for local people, distributing any leftovers to the homeless. It was all so different from England, where nuns ran schools and hospitals, in the main for the affluent. This convent was small, and so was the community: just four nuns. Inside, it was oppressively claustrophobic, but the welcome was warm and a smiling nun came bustling toward us, wiping her hands on her apron.

"Sister Superior," said Susan.

The bedrooms, where we stowed our cases, were also very small, a couple of narrow beds in each. I was initially charmed by their austerity, although even then, when I had begun to find asceticism quite appealing, it did occur to me that living in such very close proximity, in the intimacy of a bedroom, might give rise to more than a few difficulties. My bedroom at home was my own personal bolt-hole; there didn't seem to be anything very personal here.

"Are the bedrooms as small as this in the Noviciate?" I asked Susan. It had not occurred to me that I might have to share.

"I'm not sure; I haven't been upstairs in the Noviciate." She had visited the Mother House the previous summer. "I think there are dormitories, I slept in a guest room. It was bigger than this."

"Dormitories!" Once again, under all my excitement, there was a pang of trepidation and my hands felt clammy. I had not shared a bedroom since boarding school.

All activities in that small convent – meals, recreation, and work – seemed to take place in the kitchen. Apart from the bedrooms, where was the rest of it? The Sister Superior took us along a passage and opened a door.

"*Notre chapelle*," she said, and smiled. It gave out onto the street, but the noise of traffic was muted, the room shaded by pale wooden shutters. Autumn sunlight, soft and golden, filtered through and fell on the pale stone of the small altar and the two beautiful pewter candlesticks. "Cream and gold, cream and gold," I thought, then unexpectedly, "Butter and toast." The muffled street noises, the shuttered sun, the warm stone, the flickering sanctuary lamp, and the smell of wax mixed with incense were soporific and mesmerising. Sister Superior took her place at one of the prie-dieux, bowed her head, and seemed lost in prayer. Self-consciously, we followed suit. Did I pray or not? I was certainly silent and felt a little overwhelmed.

As I knelt, I gradually became aware of three sensations, none of them to do with God: I was terribly hungry, I was desperate to go to the lavatory, and the prie-dieux were horrendously uncomfortable. Thankfully, after about five minutes, and five minutes is a long time to be on one's knees in those circumstances, Sister Superior rose and we followed.

"Where's the loo?" I hissed at Susan.

I found myself in a small windowless room with a washbasin in it. There were two doors. The first revealed a cleaning cupboard: brushes, buckets, and mops. Expectantly, I opened the second and found myself looking into a small cubicle. I could not at first imagine its purpose. It was tiled, floor and walls, the floor was concave and there was a hole in the centre of it, either side of which there were two tiled footprints. It smelled strongly of bleach. The chain flush was the giveaway. I stared at it, appalled. I was wearing high heels. How could I possibly balance? What if I didn't get my aim correct? I had peed many times "al fresco", so to speak, but this primitive arrangement was in a flat, for God's sake. The blasphemy rose instinctively to my mind.

I wondered for a moment if my discomfort could be ignored. Maybe if we were going out I could find a public toilet in Paris where they had a proper lavatory. It was just as well that I didn't succumb to that idea: this was the sixties and public lavatories in France were renowned all over Europe for their unsavoury aspect.

Driven to desperation, I decided to improvise, although in fact it would have been far simpler to use the lavatory. Making sure the door was locked, and as quietly as I could, I opened the door of the cleaning cupboard. Gritting my teeth against the noise, I took out the metal bucket, turned it upside down, kicked off my high heels, clambered onto it, hoisted up my skirt, lowered my pants, and, perching on the edge of it, praying that I wouldn't bring the whole thing off the wall, urinated luxuriously into the sink.

Back in the kitchen there was a warm yeasty smell of fresh bread. Among the bread, butter, and cheese on the table was a strange, greasy, potted meat.

"Taste the rillettes." Susan pushed the pot toward me. "I know it doesn't look very appetizing, but it's lovely. Go on, try it with these small pickled cucumbers."

Gingerly I took some. It was delicious. It was followed by a rich creamy cheese with a yellow rind that Susan told me was made by the Trappists. Afterwards we had peaches and grapes. The grim memory of the "squat-down" loo began to fade.

As we had hoped, Sister Superior suggested, via the ever willing Susan, that we might like to see something of Paris before our train left that evening. Four hours was not long, but I hoped that the Eiffel Tower might be on the itinerary and would anyone come to Paris and not at least look at the outside of the Louvre? So with some enthusiasm and a heightened feeling of expectancy, I followed Susan and our pretty nun out into the street, the latter looking dubiously at my high heels.

We got off the bus outside, I was told, the Mother House of the Daughters of Charity of St Vincent de Paul. These were the sisters of the large white butterfly bonnets and the grey-blue dresses, instantly recognizable. Later they would change their habit for a modern costume of singular ugliness, completely devoid of the historical significance of the old one. Not only did this render them anonymous overnight, but this transformation made them look like frumpish pre-war nurses. In 1961, however, they were still the exotically garbed nuns of my childhood.

In the chapel, the sisters had just finished reciting the rosary. Filing out of their pews, with their starched sail-like butterfly bonnets erect, and their grey-blue dresses billowing, they looked for all the world like a flotilla of little sailing boats, the kind that children make out of paper to float on a local pond. The bonnets only flopped when it rained and then they kept them pinned together with a little clothes peg. Heaven knows what they did if it was windy.

The interior of the chapel, unlike the elegant exterior, was nineteenth century and alarmingly decorated. Niches and saints, all garishly coloured, proliferated. It was Catholic kitsch at its worst.

Bewildered, I asked, "Whatever are we here for?"

Poor Susan, who had been translating for me since we touched down, both transmitting and receiving, was beginning wilt. "To see St Catherine Labouré," she said briefly.

In a glass case, in a side chapel, lay what I took to be a wax effigy of a female figure in religious costume.

"That's really her body?" It could have been the heat, the excitement of Paris or the greasy rillettes we had had for lunch, but I felt distinctly queasy. My instinct was to recoil in horror.

"She's embalmed – you know, preserved." Painstakingly Susan explained the charming story. When Catherine Labouré was a novice, she woke up one night to hear someone calling her. Novices are not usually encouraged to wander around convents in their nighties, so she might have been expected to stay tucked up in bed, but she didn't. On a chair in the chapel was the Virgin Mary. Catherine recognized her straight away and, kneeling down beside her, put her clasped hands on the Virgin's knee. In the course of a tender conversation the Virgin Mary asked that a medal should be struck in her honour. To those who wore it, the Virgin Mary promised protection and an assurance that they would not die without receiving God's grace.

The Blessed Virgin is prone to appear in very odd places. At Fatima in Portugal she hovered over a holm oak. Details are very important in apparitions! At Pontmain and Lourdes in France she appeared respectively above a barn and in a hollow above a cave that was used as the local tip, and at Knock in Ireland she was halfway up a church wall. So this prosaic vision had a delightful domestic and human quality. It was also a very material apparition, and the Virgin's message was a loving and comforting one.

"Yes," I said, when Susan had finished the story. "Yes, I like it. She usually turns up like Cassandra, to predict some terrible tribulation, to call for repentance, and to reproach us for our failings. Why does she never appear to encourage people who beaver away for the kingdom of God? Why don't the truly good and unselfish people ever get words of praise, and why are all these heavenly manifestations so full of doom and gloom?"

"Don't ask me. Perhaps virtue is its own reward and good people don't need encouragement." Susan looked tired and her answer was almost brusque. I was unconvinced.

I stared, riveted, at the figure lying like Snow White in her glass case. Her skin was yellow and her age indeterminate. The whole thing had a terribly unreal aspect, except for the hands, which were pressed softly together, unwrinkled and as smooth as marble. I couldn't take my eyes away from them.

Questions tumbled like lottery balls in my mind: What did it feel like to put one's hands on the Virgin's knee? Was her flesh warm to the touch? Could Catherine feel her breath on her cheek? What did one ask of hands that had been so close to the Mother of God? Could you expect them to do the washing-up, to peel potatoes, to scrub and polish, to clean a lavatory, for heaven's sake? How could one relate normally to other people after such an experience? Imagine saying, *Well, as the Blessed Virgin said to me when we were together…* What sort of response would that elicit?

In a whirl of confusion I left the chapel and followed my companions out into the steamy street.

CHAPTER 2

The Furies at the Door

"Where are we off to now?" Expectation, I now decided, was overrated.

"We are going to Sacré-Coeur," said Susan obligingly. I brightened.

"Ah," I said, "that's in Montmartre." At least we were going somewhere I had heard of.

Many sneer at Sacré-Coeur, that odd exotic church high on the hill in the north of the city. Those who pride themselves on their architectural know-how point out that the domes are the wrong shape and the proportions clumsy. The church is in an inappropriate style for both the area and the city in general, and is faintly ridiculous, being more of a pastiche than a genuinely new concept. I found it wonderfully impressive, and despite its aesthetic defects I have always kept a sneaking affection for it. That hot September afternoon, looking up at its white façade from the bottom of the great flight of steps, it looked spectacular, glittering in the strong autumn sun. Once on the terrace, I was thrilled to see at last the twin towers of Notre Dame and the metal spike of the Eiffel Tower. I hung, enchanted, over the balustrade, eagerly trying to pick out all the landmarks I had read about, and followed my companions reluctantly away from such a magnificent vista.

On either side of the main door of the church, on stools so low that they appeared to be sitting on the ground, were two Carmelite nuns with begging bowls in front of them. In their coarse ungainly brown habits and heavy black veils they seemed worlds away from our neat nun in her long elegant black habit, white collar, immaculate headband, and trim veil. They looked hot and dispirited, as well they might, as there was precious little in the begging bowls. Perhaps it was the heat that accounted for the tension. It became very clear as we approached them that they were quarrelling viciously. They were glaring at each other. Even at ten yards away, the hissed invectives were clearly audible, although for me incomprehensible.

They fell silent as we passed between them, although the air was so jagged with their fury that my calves tingled and I should not have been surprised to find ladders in my stockings.

Inside, the church was a disappointment: cold, gloomy, and cavernous. I was pleased to get outside again, despite having to run the gauntlet of the furies at the door. Susan put a coin in the bowl of one as she left, whereupon the other set up the kind of mournful and plaintive keening that we associate these days with refugees from Eastern Europe.

I side-stepped around them and caught Susan's elbow. "I thought Carmelites were enclosed. Who let these two horrors out?"

"These must be extern sisters. Carmelite convents are quite small, usually only about twenty-four nuns, and there might only be three or four externs. They live separately outside the enclosure, come and go, do the shopping and that sort of thing."

"Heavens, how dreadful! That pair have probably been at each other's throats the life-long day! It must be misery for the others." I looked back over my shoulder and although I could no longer hear them, their body language indicated only too clearly that they were still quarrelling. They didn't seem to me a very good advertisement for the religious life.

By 7:00 p.m., when we left for the station, I was beginning to feel very tired indeed and Susan's translations, in both directions, were becoming monosyllabic. If I had been offered the chance, I would probably have turned tail and headed home. The station was busy. Soldiers blocked the door to our carriage. Our patient guide caught sight of a rotund little priest hurrying down the platform. Nodding to her, he pushed the soldiers aside but, before he could board the train, she collared him and introduced us in a sort of excited stage whisper as two young postulants going to enter the noviciate. He looked at us blandly and made some sort of neutral comment.

"She's asked him to keep an eye on us to make sure we don't miss the stop," said Susan. I watched him dubiously as he disappeared into a carriage. We never set eyes on him again.

As we boarded the train, the soldiers began a sniggering conversation and we were no sooner seated and I had kicked off my shoes than the door of the carriage was pushed open. One of them sat down opposite us, his mates leering at him through the window. Our pretty nun waved us off, her duty done. The soldier stared at us impassively during the entire journey. He was handsome, olive skinned, with hot, dark eyes. I leaned my head against the window and stared out into the dark. Lights in the carriage came on and, reflected in the glass, I saw the soldier looking at me. Inadvertently I caught his glance and felt ashamed because I felt flattered. He didn't remind me of any past boyfriend, and I'd had several, but I recognized the expression on his face: quizzical, slightly challenging, even flirtatious. God help me, he had seen that I was pleased. I felt shame flare in me.

I sank back in my seat and closed my eyes. I felt disembodied. Now, it seemed, everything was being done for me. For the moment I didn't need to make any decisions, but could just follow, like an automaton. Images of the day danced behind my eyelids, and I felt the beginning of a headache.

Susan took out a book and began to read. I lit a cigarette, looked at her, and wondered what she was feeling. After a while, lulled by the train, I began to drift off.

"It's the next stop." Her voice jerked me out of my reverie. Looking at the packet of cigarettes, I saw I had four left and tossed them out of the window. Sister Mistress of Novices, when she found out later, was cross, assuring me that I wouldn't have been the first postulant to be weaned off cigarettes. Entering a convent, she pointed out, was challenging enough without the added burden of overcoming an addiction. Actually I didn't find it particularly hard at all to give them up but could have enjoyed the odd one if I had had the opportunity!

The platform was dimly lit. We stood in silence, our cases beside us; it was cold and very quiet. I began to feel chilly and started to shiver from tiredness and apprehension. Minutes passed, then out of the gloom a tall rangy nun with a long loping stride came toward us, smiling.

"It's Sister Mistress of Novices," said Susan.

Outside in the station yard was a van and an odd little car. I stared in astonishment. There must have been plenty of those funny little 2CV cars in Paris, but somehow they hadn't registered at all. My impression was of something knocked up mainly from scrap metal and kitchen utensils. The headlights looked like saucepans, and its ridged bonnet and curved roof seemed to be made of sheets of corrugated iron. It took me years to get used to them and, even now, despite their jolly colours and cult image, I can never see one without being immediately transported back to that dark station yard and the bewildering feeling of being adrift in the unknown.

We rattled along through the small dark town, the narrow streets illuminated occasionally by bright and misted windows, one a bar. I looked longingly at it. A whisky would have gone down very well at that moment. I could almost taste it. We crossed a square. I saw a huge floodlit church, which I knew was the basilica, attached to the Mother House, and beyond it a pair of enormous curved wooden doors, which swung open at our approach. We bumped over cobbles under the vast porch and along a gravel terrace. An open door splashed out light. A plump, rosy-cheeked, and rather excitable nun, if the voluble greeting was anything to go by, appeared and hustled us inside, followed by Sister Mistress of Novices.

We found ourselves in a very large room, sparsely furnished with two long rows of desks and rush-seated stools. The floor was magnificent and highly polished parquet. On the end wall hung an enormous crucifix.

We followed the rotund little nun across the room. I, acutely aware of the noise of my heels, feared that the metal tips of my stilettos were doing irreparable damage to the floor. Double doors led us out into a dim corridor, with a tiled floor, whitewashed walls, and brown radiators. Bewildered, I felt like Alice looking down the long passage at the end of her fall down the rabbit hole; here too there were several doors. The house was completely silent; we could have been the only people in it. In a smallish room, milk, bread, and grapes were laid out for us. Was there a sign with "Eat me" and "Drink me" on the table? I half-expected one. I wasn't Alice, but I was certainly in another world, wonderland perhaps, diminished, overwhelmed by the huge building and high-ceilinged room. The whole thing seemed unreal.

The excitable nun, it transpired, was the Postulant Mistress, and her name was Sister Marie-Germaine. She had a warm heart and a passionate nature, and that evening she welcomed us with great kindness. She was not entirely to blame for the fact that we were never to get on. Susan, on the other hand, was to have a close and fruitful relationship with her and undoubtedly uncovered and discovered more qualities in her than I did.

By this stage, it had been a very long day; I was almost beyond any kind of interaction and longed for bed.

The dormitory was divided into cubicles containing a bed, a bedside table, and a chair, a curtain hung at the entrance. They were as impersonal as the bedrooms in the Paris convent, but at least they were separated by wooden partitions.

At one end of the room was a metal trough, and above it half a dozen brass cold water taps. There was a waste pipe but no plug. I washed my face and brushed my teeth, wondering how, in this public place, the more intimate parts could be dealt with, but I decided that I could investigate that in the morning.

Sister Marie-Germaine, who had shown us our beds, tut-tutted disapprovingly when we began to talk as we opened our cases. The welcome that we had been given was comforting and, with the resilience of youth, the moments of apprehension were forgotten. I was filled with excited anticipation – so much so that, despite my tiredness, I feared I wouldn't sleep. Sister Marie-Germaine, who was sharing our dormitory, tossed and turned in her bed for a little while and then began to snore gently. The sheets smelled of camphor and were coarse, but not unpleasantly so. I breathed in the scent of the sheets and began to say a decade of the rosary. I was asleep before I was halfway through.

In the morning we were shown to a large shower room. It was bleak but functional and echoed like a public baths. There were two cubicles containing what I took at first to be lavatories, but with no seat, lid, or chain.

"What are these for?" I asked Susan. She looked sheepish for a moment but Sister Marie-Germane interjected before she could reply, obviously understanding my interrogative.

"*Pour les pieds*," she said blandly.

"For washing your feet… and anything else that you need to wash." Susan's translation was clearly giving her some problem, and she looked uncomfortable.

"For washing your feet?" It all looked odd and I puzzled over it for a moment. I was deeply relieved to see that the lavatories looked normal. I thought again with horror of the "squat-down".

Outside the dormitory the wide landing was lined with huge linen presses. We each had a shelf and a drawer labelled with our name. It was the first time I was to see my new title in black and white, "Sister Eleanor", and on the shelf above, "Sister Susan". We smiled with delight at each other.

CHAPTER 3

A Very Big Decision

Questions, questions, questions! Over the previous months I had become so weary of answering them that I had begun to wish I had told nobody and just disappeared.

"But Eleanor, don't you want to get married?" I suppose this question was reasonable, as was, I believed, my reply: "Every girl wants to get married, don't they; but I can't get married *and* be nun, can I?"

The future was, well, just that: the future. I didn't want to look too far ahead. In any event, at eighteen it is almost impossible to imagine how one will feel at thirty; it's half a lifetime away. Few girls in the sixties had serious career ambitions; marriage and a family were the norm. "God," I was assured by many people who seemed to know more about it than I did, "would sort it all out."

"When did you first decide you wanted to be a nun?" This was the question I dreaded most, because it was so difficult to answer. Actually the idea that God was calling me to live a life dedicated to his service was not totally welcome. There were so many things that I enjoyed, even relished, about my current existence. Did I love God; did I even really know him? In a vague sort of way he had been a presence in my life for as long as I could remember, so, for better or for worse, I knew that I had to find out if this was truly "the real thing".

When indeed had it all begun to take shape? It began, I think, with a friend, David, who told me he was going to become a priest. I was stunned. This handsome nineteen-year-old boy was going to give up normal life, enter the priesthood, and become a monk into the bargain.

"Oh David, don't talk such nonsense! Sleep with a few girls and you'll soon forget about the idea." He took my coarse recommendations in good part, but he didn't forget about "the idea". He became a priest and although I was cross with him and thought it a terrible waste, it moved something in me. I became restless, and suffered from an ill-defined unease, a general feeling of dissatisfaction with my life. How did he know if he had a vocation? How could you tell? Suppose I had one; how would I know? So within a few months of David's departure, boldly, even starkly, and with no very clear idea of what should come next, I began to talk about becoming a nun.

Initially it was just a declaration of future intent. I knew what being a nun was, but it was unformed in my mind, even chaotic. What should I do next?

My parish priest was encouraging but cautious. Facing me across the table in his comfortable sitting room, he suggested gently, "It might be sensible, Eleanor, if you are serious about dedicating your life to God in the religious life, not to accept any more invitations from boyfriends – you know, dates and things."

I was horrified and stared at him aghast. "But Father, I'm going to the Balliol College Summer Ball." I was appalled at the thought of missing that. Apart from anything else, I'd bought the dress.

"Eleanor, do you really feel that you have a vocation? Do you truly think God is calling you? If you do, don't you think you could sacrifice a ball or two?"

I was irritated by the question. Of course if I *had* to, I could sacrifice a lot of things, but all the same...

"But Father, why would God want me to do that? Isn't the whole point of going into a convent to... what do they call it, 'to try a vocation', to see if it is the genuine thing? How will I know until I get in?"

I could hear myself getting both cross and defensive. This conversation, I thought, was not going the way I had hoped.

Clearly once inside I wouldn't be going to balls and parties, but there didn't seem much point in giving them up until my new life necessitated it. He was looking at me very seriously and I stared back, truculently. Then I played what I thought was my trump card.

"What about St Augustine?" I said triumphantly. "What about, 'Lord make me chaste, but not just yet'?"

He burst out laughing and in relief I laughed with him.

"You've made your point. Enjoy the ball. But I still think you should give up the dates; and," he added, "go and visit some nuns."

Some of my friends thought the whole idea hilarious, but not everybody laughed. Some were appalled, others sceptical.

Later, talking to other postulants and novices, I discovered that for every devout girl who enters a convent and has yearned to be a nun for as long as she can remember, there are many who do so almost against their inclination. It is felt as an irresistible force. Thomas Merton, the Trappist monk and well-known writer, struggled for a long time with his own calling and he was by no means unusual. St Francis of Assisi came from a wealthy, powerful family and he too initially fought against his particular vocation.

"Of course I believe in God," I said crossly to another bemused acquaintance. "I'm a Catholic. The church is important to me; I've grown up in it. I was at a convent school. I follow the Commandments... or most of them. I go to Mass... occasionally. I even go to Confession... sometimes."

But if I had been asked what difference it made on a day-to-day basis to my life, I would have been at a loss to reply. So actually I was as puzzled as my friends were. Puzzlement and a certain confusion were the dominant emotions that I was experiencing at the time. But I followed my priest's advice and sheepishly went to visit several convents. What was I looking for? I think I was looking for a match, or perhaps a sign; for a community where I would think, "This is it," or at least, "*Perhaps* this is it," and where they would say, "Yes, you're right for us; come in." Actually they all said, "Come in," as all convents were keen to recruit. This only compounded my confusion. Which one to choose?

"How do I know if I've got a vocation?" I asked a charming Franciscan nun. "I mean, how *can* I tell?"

"You can't," she replied cheerfully, "until you try it. You've got to suck it and see."

A community in Romiley, near Manchester, were instantly appealing, warm, and welcoming, and not pushy. I liked them and they appeared to like me. Certainly they took me at face value and never questioned my motives or my suitability for convent life.

Sister Anna, in charge of recruitment, told me later that like the apostles as "fishers of men", or in her case a fisher of women, she cast out her net, caught as many as she could, hauled them in, and then handed over the catch to the Sister Mistress of Novices to be sorted out, the rejects being tossed back. It was not her job, she explained as she hauled *me* in, to question the quality of what she had caught. She was the fisherman, not the quality assessor.

So my application to enter the Noviciate of the Sisters of Charity of Our Lady of Evron at the Mother House in France was ratified. There was a Noviciate in Lisdoonvarna in Ireland, but Sister Anna had already hooked one candidate who wanted to go to the French Noviciate and she was on the look-out for another. She skated suavely over Ireland and praised Evron to such an extent that I never really considered anything else, nor asked for any information about Ireland.

Although I had been accepted as an "aspirant" to the congregation, in preparation for the French adventure I was invited to spend the summer prior to going to France in their convent in Filey (a pleasant little seaside town in North East Yorkshire), presumably to see how I would shape up. A sweet elderly nun attempted to instil into me a little basic French using a ferocious grammar and the congregation's Prayer Book, called the Office Book. I was a reluctant pupil, so it was not a great success.

In fact the whole time there was unsatisfactory. I wasn't at all sure what I was supposed to be doing. The sisters were delightful and charming, and their life seemed straightforward and simple, but although I went for long walks with some of them, and they were fun and chatty, I felt I was being kept at a distance. I was not invited to participate in their community life, not even during recreation, although I could hear laughter and animated conversation. I even ate alone! So I had a great deal of time on my hands and, when I was bored in the evening, I went to the local cinema. I still didn't see any need to give up what I thought were perfectly normal and innocent pleasures before I had to. Actually I had no constraints put on me at all. I went to the community prayers, to Mass, and to Benediction, but otherwise was as free as the air to come and go as I wished. Staring out across the grey swell of the North Sea at the end of the sea wall, huddled against the wind, a cigarette cupped in my hand, I did have moments of serious doubt, and wondered whether I should just go home. I even thought about going to the pub one night. The nuns knew I was smoking, but it didn't seem to bother them. The Sister Superior, a charming, intelligent, and very spiritual woman, sometimes teased me gently: "You'll have to put all this behind you in the Noviciate, Eleanor." She took the novel I was reading from me and leafed through it. "No, there definitely won't be any more of this."

CHAPTER 4

First Impressions

Once in France, I found the language barrier was a greater difficulty than I had expected. With the insouciance of youth, I hadn't thought about it much and paid for my lack of application in Yorkshire. I would have had a hard time without my English companion, Sister Susan. She did a heroic job translating for me and when she was not with me, I struggled. Sister Marie-Germaine, for all her jollity, was singularly unsympathetic. She became quite irritated if, after several minutes, I still couldn't understand, and thought that it was my obstinacy rather than incomprehension. The English are not the only ones to believe that repeating a phrase slowly and loudly makes it more understandable.

We found, that first morning, that the refectory was another vast and austere room, with a monastic gravity about it. A jolly nun called Sister Bernadette, with wisps of dark hair escaping from her headband and wearing wellington boots, arrived with our breakfast, a copious plate of ham and eggs. We thought it a nice gesture for our first meal but began to be uneasy when it became obvious that it was to be a daily ritual.

We pointed out that bacon and eggs was usually only a weekend event in England. This met with surprising resistance. Reverend Mother General, the El Supremo of the congregation, was most anxious, we were told, to make us feel at home. She was always offered the full English breakfast on her visits to the English convents and assumed it was the norm. She usually had a working breakfast with the various Sister Superiors, so had no idea what the rest of the community were eating.

After some persistence, we prevailed and exchanged the cooked breakfast for the steaming bowls of coffee, bread and butter, and thick treacly jam made from tomatoes that everybody else was having.

Convents are big places and it is usual and sensible to give the rooms names in order to identify where people are. The novices' classroom, called Sacré-Coeur, was the room that we had crossed on our arrival the previous evening. Here we were introduced to the twenty white-veiled novices and a tall, lean, patrician-looking nun, Sister Marie-Suzanne, who was in charge of studies and was also Choir Mistress and Deputy Novice Mistress. We all looked at each other with acute curiosity and interest. This was our new community; these would be our companions, our new friends who would replace the ones we had left behind.

In everyday life you can pick and choose the people you want to spend time with. In a community you don't have that option. They fluttered around us like butterflies. While it was unnerving to be surrounded enthusiastically by strangers, it was fun too. I was young and had always been gregarious so, apart from barely understanding a word, I was enjoying myself.

They were as curious about us as we were about them, and we felt exotically foreign. Indeed it came home to us very clearly that first morning that we really were in the "French Desert", as it soon became unnervingly evident that their ignorance of anything non-Gallic was more or less total. I was dumbfounded when one tall elegant novice asked me, smiling, "Are you an Anglican?" For a moment I imagined that this peculiar question had come about because it was generally known that Sister Susan was a convert to Roman Catholicism. However, when I said no, she looked taken aback, saying that she thought the English were all Anglicans. When Sister Susan pointed out that we had to be Roman Catholics to join a Roman Catholic religious organization, we were asked naïvely: "Aren't Anglicans Christians then?"

There was worse to come. The patrician-looking nun, who had looked increasingly grim during this exchange, said she would explain it all later and that Anglicans, like all Protestants, were heretics, and heretics didn't become nuns. She was wrong, of course, but it seemed inappropriate to tell her. Poor Sister Susan looked stunned by this intemperate description of Protestants.

After leaving Sacré-Coeur, we had five minutes of Sister Marie-Germaine scolding us and regretting the bad impression we had made, and then she seemed to forget about the whole episode. I felt irritated that I had not been able to explain.

"We'll get used to it. There is going to be a lot more of it," said Sister Susan. She was right.

The next few days were novel and interesting, but utterly exhausting. Trying to follow what is being said in any foreign language is tiring, even if only for a couple of hours. We were subjected to it all day and, after twenty-four hours' grace, were positively discouraged from speaking English together. This caused both of us pain and difficulty. There were so many questions that I couldn't ask because I lacked the linguistic tools. So often, I felt bewildered, lost, and not a little frightened.

I wrestled with the foreign language, but also with a completely new way of life, new concepts, and a new value system. We fell into bed at night light-headed with fatigue and plunged into oblivion, only to get up bleary-eyed at 7:00 a.m. for 7:30 a.m. Mass, our brains still buzzing. This relatively late getting-up time was a concession. We were not yet officially part of the congregation: we were still "aspirants". We wondered how we would ever manage the 6:00 a.m. rising bell of the postulants and hardly dared think about the 5:30 a.m. start to the day that was the norm for the professed nuns and the novices.

The compensation was the beauty of the chapel, the reassuring familiarity of the Latin Mass, and the spine-tingling purity of the Office, the communal prayer of the community, chanted by sixty nuns and novices. The lovely movement of the alternating verses moved back and forth between the two sides of the choir. The first line of each psalm was intoned by a single voice and then the whole was taken up by the group. It filled me with a tremendous longing to be a part of it all. I felt as if my soul was flowering, as if something was swelling inside me that might burst out at any time. It felt uncontrollable. When, later in life, I tried to explain it to a friend, she said irreverently, "What, like in the film *Alien?*" And although I laughed it was a remarkably good analogy, for I did feel as if I had been invaded. I gave myself over to it completely; I couldn't get enough of it.

However, these were the high spots. Our days were empty and seemed at least thirty-six hours long. We were rarely left alone; Sister Marie-Germaine accompanied us everywhere. Apart from the two periods of recreation, we saw little of the novices. I had nothing to read, as all books were in French, and there was no radio. We became steadily more bored. Once again, as in Yorkshire, nothing structured seemed to have been planned for us.

"Confession," announced Sister Marie-Germaine one day, as if it were a treat, and whisked us off in the little van to Laval, a nearby town. Our English-speaking confessor was a suave and sophisticated Jesuit who had little time for "the good sisters". I didn't actually feel that I had any sins to confess but went through the motions anyway. Was getting cross a sin? I couldn't remember, and some of my character defects, my enjoyment of gossip no matter how malicious, and my almost total inability to keep a secret, were not actually a part of my new life. There were no young men to lust after either – not that I missed them; I was too tired. The rough red wine or even rougher cider on the table at mealtimes held no real appeal. I expect the good Jesuit thought me a vapid penitent.

One cheering thing did come out of this dull little trip: we were able to borrow some English books. Of all the things that I missed, books were by far the most significant. I had always been a voracious reader.

The Jesuits' library was extensive. I didn't feel that I was ready for Thomas Aquinas, and neither did the Jesuit, judging by his curling lip when innocently I asked him if he thought I would enjoy it.

"It's arduous," he replied sardonically. However, he pulled down *The Hidden Face* by Ida Gorres, a book that I did subsequently enjoy very much. It was a biography of St Thérèse of Lisieux, the Carmelite nun. She had a grim time of it, being at the centre of a power struggle between her siblings, who were nuns in the Carmel monastery with her, and the gifted but unbalanced prioress. I remembered the two Carmelite harridans I had seen outside the church in Paris. Thérèse died of generalized TB aged twenty-four, due to a regime that confused deprivation and wanton neglect with austerity and asceticism. Beneath the sometimes toe-curling sentimentality of her nineteenth-century piety, or at least the expression of it, was a deep and heroic spirituality. From the time she entered Carmel until her death less than a decade later, she transformed herself from an over-indulged little adolescent with a marked tendency to neurosis into a mature, self-possessed young woman: one, furthermore, who understood with singular clarity that the essence of religious life was to do the ordinary as if it were the extraordinary, and that the road to perfection was paved with the minutia of the everyday. I became deeply enthralled by her and she was to be a reference point for me in many day-to-day events.

Among all the serious tomes, I saw, incongruously, a cheap, pale blue, modern-looking binding and grabbed it in passing. It was a collection of Damon Runyon stories. I had enjoyed *Guys and Dolls*, and thought his tales of hoodlums and prohibition and dashing villains and tarts with hearts of gold in the America of the thirties were great. As nobody else in the Noviciate spoke English, apart from Sister Susan, nobody knew what I was reading. The light relief it offered was a great help.

Between outings and Confession, we explored the grounds, which were extensive. Formal parterres once filled with flowers and still surrounded by neat box hedges had been turned over to vegetable plots. Beyond the gardens were apple orchards and beyond them and around the perimeter ran long avenues of hornbeam called *charmilles*. Within the complex of the Mother House, a beautiful seventeenth-century building that had once been a Benedictine monastery leased to the congregation since the time of Napoleon, were a domestic science school and a small unit for severely handicapped children. We used to see them sometimes in the garden and we could always hear their inarticulate cries from behind the high wall that surrounded the building. There was a laundry, a bakery, and a small farm with chickens and turkeys. We thought there must have been a cow, as the milk that came to the refectory for our afternoon tea, a concession to our Englishness, brought in cheerfully and noisily by the wellington-wearing sister, was occasionally gritty and sometimes streaked with what we hoped was mud!

"What is this?" I asked Sister Susan, staring dubiously down at the brown flecks floating on the top of the milk.

"It's because the udders haven't been washed. We can go up to St Luke the sick-room and get some cotton-wool balls and strain the milk through." I was impressed by her know-how. The amount of dirt left behind was alarming and the cotton wool made the milk taste chalky, but we felt that it was cleaner and it was certainly whiter.

"I'm learning new things every day."

"Yes – like the provenance of the black pudding." Sister Susan shuddered at the memory.

CHAPTER 5

Black Pudding

The black pudding episode became a euphemism for everything that we found strange. "It's black pudding," we'd say to each other when faced with imponderables, and yet the episode had arisen in humdrum circumstances.

"Could we go for a walk in the town?" Our request for what seemed a very innocent and reasonable activity was met with such a stark and horrified refusal, we felt our request was morally suspect. However, it did get us yet more trips in the van. Whenever Sister Marie-Germaine went out, we accompanied her, visiting many of our little convents. She showed us off and introduced us like a proud mother. Our trips were not uneventful, however. Sister Susan, who had a deep-rooted and pathological fear of birds and feathers, turned grey with horror and cowered in a corner before succumbing quite seriously to hysterics in one friendly convent, when the Sister Superior tried to take a cockatoo out of its cage. The poor woman clearly felt that if she could only get her trembling visitor to stroke the little bird or perhaps allow it to perch on her finger, she would not be so afraid. It was an alarming episode, terror on one side and total incomprehension on the other. When the bird was safely back in its cage, poor Sister Susan calmed down.

"How long have you had this feather phobia? Were you frightened by a bird in your pram?" I was intrigued, as I had never seen anyone have hysterics before.

"I've always had it. If I find a feather on my bed that may have escaped from my pillow, I can only pick it up with a hanky." She was still shaking.

I had my dramas too and burst into tears when, unexpectedly, the theme tune of *The Archers* floated out, as an equally kindly nun tried, obviously with some success, to tune her radio to an English wavelength.

"I don't even like *The Archers*," I wept.

"It's homesickness," said Sister Susan comfortingly.

The last outing before our formal admission to the noviciate was memorable. Late one evening, our van driver turned down a narrow country lane and stopped outside a small cottage with some outbuildings behind it. Our driver got out, as did Sister Marie-Germaine. We could see her chatting away animatedly to a woman who had come to the door. We sat in companionable silence for a moment, then I said, "Shall we say our rosary?"

"Oh yes," said Sister Susan. "We can say it in English for a change; that'll be nice."

It was warm in the cab and the light from the open door was warm. The voices rising and falling, the bursts of sudden laughter were all reassuring and homely. I felt very happy.

"Hail Mary, full of grace, the Lord is with thee."

The beads slipped through our warm fingers. Suddenly there was the most appalling squeal, followed by a second, and then a prolonged sort of bubbling gurgle. We heard men's voices shouting. I dropped my rosary in fright. Sister Susan looked frozen to her seat. Outside the van, the two women glanced over their shoulders and then after a slight pause continued their conversation as if nothing had happened. We stared appalled at each other and then tremblingly continued...

"Holy Mary, Mother of God... What the hell was that?"

"Don't swear," replied Sister Susan automatically. Then turning a pale face toward me and taking a deep breath, said, "I think they were killing a pig."

The van driver reappeared, carrying a covered pail that he put into the back of the van. Sister Marie-Germaine clambered back into the cab and we set off, driving very slowly. Our query as to the contents of the pail confirmed our suspicion. This was a quid pro quo arrangement. The community's van driver killed the pig for the farmer and the community got the blood. The sister in charge of the kitchen made superb black pudding, we were told. There was in fact a municipal abattoir in the area but, as Sister Marie-Germaine pointed out, it was an expensive business for a smallholder with one pig. If you had several animals well and good, but one pig cost too much money and our van driver was used to it; he did it every year.

"But it's *cruel*!" I expostulated.

"How is it cruel?" She was outraged. "The pig has a wonderful life: it's spoiled by the family when it's small, has all the titbits and good food, and, at the end of its life, two or three weeks in the cider apple orchard eating as much as it wants. No wonder its flesh is so sweet. Then just one pain and it's all over."

Although we felt that we had the moral high ground, our Englishness was so obviously in conflict with Gallic behaviour that we were silent. I felt a long way from home. However, our dismay at what we thought were barbaric practices did not prevent us from eating the black pudding with relish when it was served at supper a few days later. But it took both of us some time to forget the bloodcurdling squeals of the pig.

CHAPTER 6

A Real Beginning

The eventual arrival of eight other aspirants meant that we too became a little community. I was instantly drawn to Odette, the first to arrive, although I soon learned that her sharp tongue and prickly temperament were not always easy to deal with. She had grown up in Vietnam and there was something Asiatic about her olive skin and sleek black hair. She spoke bitterly once to me about Pierre Mendès-France, the prime minister responsible for withdrawing troops from Vietnam, whose policies she said had betrayed both the Vietnamese and the French. I think her own family had suffered. I used to tell her teasingly that with her oval face, brown skin, and dark hair, she looked not unlike Juliette Gréco – the sultry singer with a long curtain of black hair, so well known in the fifties and sixties – and although she replied brusquely, I sensed she was quite flattered.

Odile, Paule, and Thérèse were the next to join. Paule came from a large family. Her father was a forester and her description of the family home made it sound like something out of Hansel and Gretel. We were then joined by Renée, Yvonne, and Agnès. The latter was a lovely, cheerful, slow-moving woman, with a weather-beaten face and bright blue eyes. Annie, the last, came a full week after the official entry. She was a Parisienne; from Versailles actually, but she always said she was a Parisienne. She was extremely pretty, blonde, and bubbly. At regular intervals during the postulancy, she had to return to Paris to see her doctor for some unspecified illness. She never told us what it was and we were too polite to ask, but in our enclosed little world where even the most personal and intimate events were common knowledge, her repeated absences and the secrecy that surrounded them caused irritation.

One morning I woke up with the sort of excitement in the pit of the stomach that one feels before a really big event. It was 1 November, the Feast of All Saints, the day of our official entry into the noviciate. After breakfast we put on our postulant clothing: black stockings, black dress, white collar, black veil attached to white Alice band. It was like getting ready for a birthday party. We were ridiculously excited. Ten grown women joyfully putting on the most uncomfortable and unbecoming clothes we had ever worn. But at last we would have proper status – we would be postulants!

I was irritated to discover that Sister Susan and I were the only two who had followed the directives that we had been sent in our uniform list regarding underwear. I had spent an inordinate amount of time and suffered embarrassment trying to find long-sleeved vests, "knickers" and nightdresses made of a material called interlock, and eventually ran them to earth in the sort of old-fashioned drapers that looked as if it were part of a film set for one of those grim fifties kitchen sink dramas. It was unpleasant fabric, a sort of cotton jersey. The hirsute shop assistant, who smelled strongly of wintergreen, evinced absolutely no surprise that a reasonably slim and attractive eighteen-year-old should be buying garments of such unrelieved ugliness. I made the mistake of showing them to my parents. My mother laughed, but my father looked horrified and poured a very serious whisky for me and an even more serious one for him, saying he hoped I knew what I was doing. Either the French candidates had been sent a different list or they had ignored it, but we certainly didn't see anyone else in interlock that morning.

In Reverend Mother General's large study we knelt in a semicircle on the floor. Over six feet tall, the Reverend Mother General was an imposing woman whose presence alone generated its own solemnity and we felt it a solemn occasion. One by one we made our request to be admitted as postulants to the congregation. I stumbled haltingly through mine. The two Mother Assistants, her councillors, smiled encouragingly, but the Reverend Mother General was impassive. I later found out that her "gravitas" covered the fact that she was a singularly humourless woman, but that day I was aware only of her aura of dignity and serenity. When she placed her hands on my head in blessing, I felt a great privilege and honour had been conferred, as indeed it had.

The rest of the day was one of celebration. At lunch there was sparkling cider, as opposed to the still, potent, opaque, and very "rough" drink with bits of bruised apple suspended in it that was usually served, and there was white wine as well as red. Normally meals were eaten in silence, with a novice reading from the lectern high up on the wall above us. It would be a biography of a saint or some local news about diocesan affairs. The only exceptions were feast days or some momentous event worthy of generalized conversation. So there was no reading during the meal that day either, as we were given permission to talk. The big change was that all the dishes that came to the table, instead of being passed around, were placed in front of Sister Marie-Germaine, who took up a large serving spoon and proceeded to dish our meal up to us, ignoring all requests for specific portion size. This in fact was the shape of things to come. She served, we accepted with good or bad grace, and then ate. In fact the "shape of things to come" was a very apposite description, as I increased from a slim size 10 to a very rotund size 16 in six months.

The personal meeting in the afternoon with Sister Mistress of Novices was miserably unsatisfactory. We smiled a lot at each other. When I understood that she was asking me why I had chosen the congregation, unhappily my linguistic abilities let me down, as did my nervousness, for I found her intimidating, so stumbled over the words in my efforts to explain my strong but incoherent "feeling" about why it had to be them rather than anyone else. Instead I said haltingly, "*Parce ce que l'habit est joli*" (Because the habit is pretty). Her ice-blue eyes stared at me for a moment, then her lips twitched and she made that most French of comments, "*Tiens*" (which can mean anything from "so" to "really" or "fancy" and can express astonishment or even outrage). It was a deeply frustrating interview.

The novices put on a little show for us after supper at recreation: songs, a recitation or two, a recorder duet, and a hilarious detailing of dos and don'ts if we wanted to get through the next six months successfully. It was recommended, rather maliciously, that we glue our veils to our head for the duration; they pinched our ears and regularly slipped off. "Sniggering" was also recommended. Postulants and even novices are subject to those uncontrollable fits of hilarity triggered by apparently completely innocuous events, so they were speaking from personal experience. "Try not to break things" was another bright suggestion, as like the Carmelites, all broken objects would be strung around our necks for a given period of time. This was quite untrue, but I had a bad moment when my bed collapsed under me one evening!

In bed, I lay awake a long time listening to the clock on the basilica chiming every quarter. Pictures, images, and memories of the day flashed past behind my closed eyes and tugged at my mind like kites in the wind. At last I tumbled into a deep but restless sleep. My last waking thought was, "I'm in!"

CHAPTER 7

Learning the Ropes

"What do you mean, 'separated from the novices'?"

"I'm just telling you what Sister Marie-Germaine said after breakfast. I knew you hadn't understood. You know the novices don't have any interaction with sisters in the Mother House? Well, we aren't supposed to have any social interaction with the novices, so we don't pick up any bad habits, I suppose; you know, like new army recruits don't mix with other soldiers till their training is finished."

Sister Susan's explanation left me dismayed. It wasn't really an issue for the rest of the postulants, who didn't know the novices, but we had begun to enjoy their company at evening recreation. "How's that going to work? We live in the same building and have recreation in the same room."

"Well, I suppose we just stay in our own little circle; after all, it's a big enough room." She smiled at my sceptical expression. "We get a Guardian Angel though!"

And so we did. Each of us was linked with a novice, whose specific task was to help us find our feet and generally to ease things along. When the Guardian Angels were allocated, I was linked with a tall, serious novice. She was pleasant if reserved, but had one major drawback: she suffered from the most appalling halitosis. It made any interaction with her a trial of endurance. She was most anxious to help, which could have been useful, particularly as she actually spoke a little English, invariably very close to my face. We never really got further than trivialities, as in the main I was keen to distance myself from her. She must have thought me rude and arrogant, and I would see her looking puzzled and hurt when it was plain I was avoiding her.

I had hoped for another novice, a big, jolly young woman, whom I liked. She had been a committed trade unionist before entering the Noviciate. She was quite a revolutionary in her way and believed that the church should be spearheading social change, not fighting to maintain the status quo. Was I in a hotbed of socialism, I wondered? I wasn't far wrong, for the congregation had been founded in the seventeenth century by a widow whose calling was the education of poor children in rural areas and the care of the sick, elderly, and destitute. Socially and politically, the congregation was essentially rural working class and it was from this environment that most of the entrants came. Even when it opened highly regarded secondary schools, some with boarders, which helped to fund smaller, poorer houses, it retained its working-class ethos. Politically it was therefore equally divided between the right-wing conservatism so common in the countryside and a more urban left-wing political tendency. The little tenement convent in Paris slotted perfectly into this mould.

We began our postulant training, and the excitement of the first few days began to evaporate as we got to grips with the reality of convent life. The first six months were hard for everyone; nobody sailed through without a qualm. I thought I loved God and was privileged to have been "called", but the change of lifestyle and the adaptation to and assimilation of a new value system were challenging. Sometimes in chapel, knowing that I was actually a part of the community life, I found myself almost overwhelmed by feelings of unreality. How had I ended up here and what exactly was I doing? Many of my companions voiced the same sentiments.

"I've always wanted to serve God as a nun," one of the postulants confided. She sighed and looked wistful. "I just didn't think it would be... I don't know... quite like this. It's not that I'm unhappy," she added hastily. "It's just not what I expected."

Some found the change in lifestyle physically taxing. Some even stopped menstruating. Eating disorders were not uncommon. Insomnia was sometimes a problem. These were not initially issues for me, although the quantity of food gave me indigestion and later I too had difficulty sleeping.

The first thing that we had to adapt to was silence. I learned not to chatter, to open and close doors quietly, and to be generally less heavy handed and noisy, but with all the new input my brain fizzed like a ginger-beer plant and I was as jumpy as a kitten. Convent life in the sixties, and not just in the Noviciate, was lived in an atmosphere of quiet. The house was hushed. This blanket of silence felt oppressive. "Quietly; quietly!" Washing-up, doing the housework, laying the table, opening and closing doors and desk lids, Sister Marie-Germaine's admonitions followed us everywhere.

"It's not possible to do the washing-up without clattering the pans *sometimes*." Sister Odette's protest got a frosty glance and a repeated "*Quietly*".

Even the most self-effacing postulant had come from a brisk, noisy, and rush-about society. Sister Paule, despite her tranquil and apparently idyllic life in a forester's cottage, came from a big noisy family in which people called out to each other, let doors slam, and participated in loud vocal exchanges. We were all used to the sound of traffic, to radio, to pop music, as a continuous background to our lives, so the stillness was, initially, a terrible constraint; at least I found it so. In its application it meant that apart from the formal community prayer and the two daily periods of recreation, we kept a rule of silence. Actually it was not nearly as hard as it sounds, even for someone as loquacious as me. If nobody else is talking, then one tends to be silent oneself. We could and did talk, but conversation was circumscribed and quiet. If you saw someone upset, unhappy, unwell, or about to make a mistake, you spoke to them. If you had to ask a question, take a message, answer the phone, participate in class discussion, you spoke. If you were a nurse, a teacher, a cook, a social worker, a carer, you were obliged to speak, and this applied even during the Great Silence, the period between the end of evening recreation and breakfast the following day, when we were free from distractions and able to concentrate on our inner life and our relationship with God. Clearly, talking was not the same thing as chatting. There was real effort involved in remembering all this. It often felt so unnatural; it was a struggle and I sometimes felt bubbles of real rebelliousness welling up.

But it was interior silence that evaded me. "God speaks to man in the stillness of his heart. Be still and know that I am God." This was the principle that underpinned the struggle to empty the mind of extraneous noise. I found it hard to silence the cacophony of sounds inside my head, yet I knew that until I had some control over my interior babble, there was little chance of my understanding what Sister Marie Germaine told me, brusquely, was God's plan for me. She seemed fairly sceptical about it.

There were other "recommendations" that I knew were in fact obligations. "You must learn to put a guard on the eyes: they are the mirror of the soul," our Postulant Mistress told us firmly. "Your eyes should be lowered when they are not being used for a specific purpose. There are many beautiful things you *can* look at, but it is never appropriate for you to be peering around inquisitively, especially if you are outside. You in particular, Sister Eleanor, could do with blinkers, and there is insolence about you when I am addressing you."

Her reproaches, as usual, both depressed and irritated me. No matter how hard I tried, I always seemed to be getting something wrong.

"We aren't supposed to look at Sister Marie-Germaine when she's telling us off; we're supposed to keep our eyes down." Sister Susan's whispered information fell on stony ground.

At recreation, holding a skein of wool for her as she rolled it into a ball, I said, "All my life, teachers, parents, authority figures have said, 'Look at me when I'm talking to you.' You are *expected* to look people in the face. To say of somebody that they would never meet your eyes is a criticism, so to stand with downcast eyes when she talks to me, particularly if it's to tick me off, which it usually is, makes me feel subservient and humiliated."

"Well," Susan grinned at me, "that's the way it's done."

My relationship with Sister Marie-Germaine began to go downhill almost straight away. The first morning after we had been received into the postulancy, she laid down the ground rules relating to the use of the shower room. The bidets we could use whenever we wanted in the evening. We could have a shower or bath once a fortnight during the afternoon and we were to come to her to ask permission, although she assured us it would always be given. Our hair could be washed once a month. Sister Susan and I had been left to our own devices before the other postulants arrived, so this total limitation of our freedom as to where and when we washed seemed outrageous. Sister Susan's gasp of horror was echoed by Sister Odette: "But at home I had a bath every day and sometimes twice a day." Sister Susan looked on the verge of tears.

"Ridiculous," was the riposte.

In the early sixties, there were still many cottages in rural France without running water, so for some of the postulants having even a mains water supply and minimal central heating was an unaccustomed luxury. They weren't going to complain about a hot fortnightly shower.

After some heated discussion and a referral to Sister Mistress of Novices, we were all allowed a weekly bath and a fortnightly hair wash. This did little to endear us to Sister Marie-Germaine, who saw us as having stirred up a hornet's nest. But there was worse to come.

I had brought with me several packets of sanitary towels, and was beginning to wonder how I would acquire more, when a pile of small neatly labelled face-cloth size towels, about a dozen of them, appeared on my shelf in the clothes press on the landing. There was a loop at each end.

"They're sanitary towels." Sister Susan's explanation left me open-mouthed with horror. This was far, far worse than the squat-down loos. I didn't even object to the fact that one of my beautiful bath towels had been sacrificed for this archaic practice. I just couldn't believe that in 1961, even in the depths of rural France, sanitary towels were being recycled.

"God, I can't cope with this," I said. "They'll have to make an exception." Then I had another ghastly thought: "Don't tell me they do this in England. This must be a French thing."

"Well," Sister Susan looked sceptical, "they won't make an exception and I've no idea if they do this in England. Didn't Sister Anna warn you?"

"Of course she didn't warn me, or I'd have brought a case load of my own and got my mother to send me more." I was quivering with horror. "Is Sister Anna the kind of nun... is any nun the kind of nun that talks about anything as personal as sanitary protection?" Another thought struck me. "How do we get them clean? Do we wash them? What happens?"

"No, I think they all go to the laundry. There's a sack somewhere in the attic. It's not that bad; we'll get used to it. It's just women together."

I never did get used to it and thankfully, as I later learned, it wasn't done in England. The "little towels", as they were called, came back from the laundry immaculately white and fluffy, but I would have exchanged all their whiteness and fluffiness for a simple packet of Dr White's.

Sister Annie, probably the most "worldly" of the postulants, was also appalled. This pretty blonde was lively and full of fun; unfortunately she could also be quite pretentious, so we often found her intensely irritating. All her gestures were over-dramatic and charged with a sort of emotionalism. In chapel she would gaze with misty-eyed intensity at the tabernacle, her head a little on one side as if rapt in prayer. To be fair she probably was, but it just looked so staged. She managed to irritate us beyond belief. She was in every way "singular", setting herself apart from the group, and being voluntarily different. Even her table manners differentiated her from the others.

"Why can't she eat normally?" complained Sister Paule, looking at Sister Annie's crooked little finger.

We all had problems with the butter. Heavily salted, it arrived fresh to the table on Sunday, but as there was no fridge in the Noviciate, it was scooped back into an earthenware pot after each meal and returned to the relative cool of the "cave". In the winter this worked very well, but in the heat of the Mayenne summer, it became increasingly rancid and by Saturday needed a lot of jam to disguise its tainted odour and taste. It wasn't inedible, just unpleasant. Sister Annie made a great fuss about it, sighing heavily and spreading an infinitesimal amount on her bread with a look that seemed to imply, "This sort of thing may be acceptable to you, but I'm not used to it at all."

We all had our own cutlery, wrapped in a table napkin that we kept in a drawer at our place. At the end of the meal, a bowl of hot water was brought to the table and we rinsed our utensils before drying them and putting them away. It may have been practical, but it wasn't very hygienic. I thought it quite fun, although the water would have benefited from some washing-up liquid, a product incidentally completely unknown in the Noviciate. Poor Sister Annie made a great song and dance about it and if the meal had been particularly greasy, she spent twice as long as the rest of us washing and polishing.

I quite liked her, although I found some of her more excessive gestures and her general self-obsession a little trying. Sister Odette couldn't stand her. She herself was desperately keen, when eventually she became a nun, to go to one of our missionary convents on the Ivory Coast. Having been brought up in Vietnam, she had a much more practical understanding of what life in an unhealthy climate and an alien culture was like, and needed to draw on all her reserves of charity and tolerance to be even civil to Sister Annie. Her sewing needle flashing like a tiny silver dagger as she stabbed it at the material she was hemming, her head bent over her work, her lips tightly compressed, she would listen in furious silence to Annie's romantic eulogizing about the African mission.

These opinions owed more to an old colonial and imperialist view than to the then current attitudes. Nuns no longer taught small African girls to make lace and recite verses of the poetry of La Fontaine, and were more into finding clean water and carrying out an intensive vaccination programme. Sister Annie's views were almost a throwback to the "Ladder to Jesus" chart in my kindergarten, which gave an especially "good little girl" the chance to win a point, enabling a little "black baby" (we each had our own) to be pinned a further step up the ladder toward baptism. Smiling, shiny black-faced cut-outs were pinned at various stages on the felt ladder. If one was a naughty little girl, they came back down one or two steps. Sadly my poor little black baby was never baptized; rather, he yo-yoed so consistently that he barely moved up or down at all. A classmate of mine was so good, she had three little babies baptized in the same week and almost undid me with envy when the headmistress, in front of the whole school, rewarded her with a holy picture! Sister Annie's attitude towards "*les petits noirs*" brought it all back to me.

In the main we were largely a united and harmonious group. I was the youngest and I think some of the older ones made allowances for me and even covered up things that might have earned me a scolding. Coming into the refectory one morning, where I was cheerfully humming while sweeping the floor, banging the brush carelessly against the table legs, Sister Renée took it quietly from my hand and gave me hers.

"What's the matter?" I asked with some surprise. "Is yours better?"

"I think you'll find it quieter," she replied, "and it doesn't need singing to." I rolled my eyes, blushed and swept carefully and quietly. Clearly I had forgotten about the rule of silence that morning.

The first letter I received after becoming a postulant had been slit open. Puzzled, I asked Sister Marie-Germaine in my ragged French if it was a mistake.

"Oh no," she said. "Sister Mistress of Novices reads all your mail." She seemed to believe we would accept this placidly, without question. Her explanation, that it was so we could be warned in advance of bad news from home, didn't ring true in the light of our obligation to leave outgoing mail unsealed as well. I was much happier with Sister Mistress of Novices' direct statement that it was an exercise in submission and humility.

What we found most difficult in our Postulant Mistress was her volatile nature. She could be charmingly amusing and even sympathetic on occasions but was often petty and obtuse. However, the aspect to her behaviour that most took us aback was her flirtatiousness. We were more embarrassed than scandalized at her demeanour when men were about. Sister Susan and I had laughed when we saw how pink and excited she became every time she needed to speak to them and thought she might become more circumspect when the other postulants arrived, but she was even worse, almost as if a larger audience was a spur to her coquetry. She couldn't hear a man in the corridor without rushing out to see what was happening. Sitting at our desks, we could hear her chatting away animatedly, her conversation punctuated by coy and teasing questions and jocular comments. It did nothing to inspire our respect, and even affable Sister Agnès was mildly critical. Sister Thérèse, whose nervous temperament predisposed her to sudden verbal outbursts, gave way to great guffaws of laughter every time Sister Marie-Germaine rose and left the room to check on the workmen's progress.

But there was another issue with her that caused us some disquiet. Gradually we became aware of obvious tension in her relationship with Sister Mistress of Novices. She found it impossible to hide her dislike or even resentment. Reverend Mother General had been the previous Novice Mistress and Sister Marie-Germaine was devoted to her, so any change in noviciate life initiated by the new incumbent, any innovation, any departure from previous practices was viewed with the deepest suspicion. Her loyalty had become a burden and she was often bitter in her comments about new institutions. If she had been able to overcome this on a day-to-day basis, both those good women could have worked productively together.

To give Sister Marie-Germaine credit, she was hardworking and experienced in religious life; she knew the ropes and her classes were well prepared. We had to learn our way around the heavy fine-paged Office Book, with its variations according to the day or liturgical period. Here she was patient and helpful. She was at her best in situations where she felt most confident and wasn't being challenged.

We rose at 6:00 a.m., so we missed Laudes, the first communal prayer of the day, in the Mother House chapel. Instead, we chanted this Office, not very harmoniously, with Sister Marie-Germaine and sometimes Sister Eugenie, the Sewing Mistress, in the Noviciate chapel. Laudes was followed by fifteen minutes of guided meditation led by Sister Marie-Germaine, the full half hour being considered a bit taxing for postulants. We were given a text or topic or quotation and then asked to consider it. It was usually either from the liturgy of the day, or, more often, a text from the New Testament: the semon on the mount; the wedding feast at Cana; Jesus at the well with the Samaritan woman. What did we understand by "living waters"? What did "poor in spirit" imply? Sister Marie-Germaine did it very well. Sitting with closed eyes, the mellow smell of polish in my nose, the soft breathing of my companions around me, her words dropped like water into the silence, limpid and fresh, the shrill voice calm. It was the only time I felt this agitated and agitating woman was at peace.

CHAPTER 8

Secrets and Mysteries

Three weeks after Sister Annie joined us, one member of our little postulant group, Sister Yvonne, disappeared. Actually we had hardly noticed her presence at all. All the other postulants, I thought, had personalities of their own, but Yvonne was faceless and seemed to have passed into our lives and out again unnoticed. We weren't even aware she had gone until Sister Mistress of Novices came into Bethlehem, the postulants' classroom, after breakfast.

"One of your companions, Yvonne, has returned to her family," she announced urbanely. "There is no need for you to worry or be concerned." She smiled reassuringly and was gone.

We were not in the least reassured and stared at each other in consternation. This surreptitious departure unnerved us all and when Sister Marie-Germaine went out on one of her periodic forays to flirt with the workmen, irrespective of the rule of silence we began an animated whispered discussion.

"Did she go last night, in the middle of the night?"

"What had she done that we couldn't say goodbye to her?"

"Did she ask to go? Was she sent away?"

"Didn't anybody hear anything? Surely someone heard something."

"I think she went after recreation, when we were in chapel. I don't remember seeing her in the dormitory."

"Maybe she was unhappy." This gentle comment from kind Sister Agnès silenced us. But the interjection didn't do much for me; I felt seriously anxious. The important question, I thought, and much more significant, was: Had she been sent away? What did you have to do that was so awful that you were dispatched before barely a month had elapsed? And a second thought surged up in my mind and made me tremble: What did you have to do to avoid it? None of us had the courage to ask either Sister Marie-Germaine or Sister Mistress of Novices for further explanation. We never did discover the reason for her abrupt departure.

It was the mystery that we found difficult: it seemed so unnecessary. We should not have been surprised. Convents in those days cloaked themselves in Masonic-like secrecy. The arrival of new candidates was openly discussed, but the departure of even a postulant who, after all, had made no commitment, was a real hole-in-the-corner affair. Professed nuns who chose to leave at the expiry of temporary vows, which they were perfectly entitled to do, were spoken of in hushed tones as if they had died. Those who requested to have their vows annulled were considered quite beyond the pale. They passed into oblivion and had no further contact with the congregation.

Some braver or less obedient souls defied this convention and managed to keep in touch, but it was a risky business. This attitude changed later on, but in the sixties it was another matter. One sister who left her convent in Liverpool managed to contact a friend still in community and arranged to meet briefly over coffee. In the bus on their way home to their respective destinations, they were horrified to find themselves at traffic lights alongside a car driven by the Mother Provincial, head of the English communities, and her secretary. Although they giggled like school children, they knew it was no laughing matter. They sank down in their seats until only the tops of their heads would have been visible and prayed that neither nun would glance to her right. Thankfully, they didn't.

This almost obsessional secrecy was applied to nearly all aspects of the religious life. We were forbidden to divulge anything in the three little books that made up the "Rule" although the "Constitutions" did little more than detail the structure and government of the congregation. One would have thought they contained seditious material instead of being documents of the most unimpeachable sobriety.

In France, they did at least have a practical attitude to money. Sister Anna, who recruited me, apparently lived on such a high spiritual plane that she quite forgot to mention what it might cost my parents to keep me for three years in an institution where expenses obviously had to be subsumed by somebody. I don't know what was said to Sister Susan, but costs were never mentioned to me. I naïvely assumed that they would be so pleased to have me that, apart from the £30 dowry (in today's money well over £300) that was mandatory, all the rest would be free. I looked blank when I heard Sister Mistress of Novices mention fees. I couldn't think what she was talking about and had to confess, with some embarrassment, that my parents, who were permanently strapped for cash, would be almost as dismayed as I was. In the event they paid up willingly, but I was furious that neither I nor they had been warned.

There were other secrets too. Every fortnight the novices had a meeting, usually held in Sister Mistress of Novices' bright and sunny anteroom; occasionally they all disappeared to join the professed nuns in the Chapter room of the Mother House.

Sister Annie enlightened us. "It's the Chapter of Faults. In front of the whole community, you have to declare the times you have broken the Rule. It's like Confession, except it's not sins." She was often a source of information; she had been friendly with the pretty nun who had taken us out in Paris. Most of us were sceptical, believing, erroneously as it turned out, that this practice was restricted to the austere lives of the contemplatives and enclosed orders.

We decided to tackle our "Guardian Angels" about it, but they clammed up immediately and referred us to Sister Marie-Germaine, who at first laughingly denied it. When challenged, she said very repressively that we would learn all about it in good time. As indeed we did.

We came across other practices that were equally startling and unexpected. A novice arriving late for dinner accidentally let the door slam. To our astonishment, she fell to her knees and kissed the floor. Kissing the floor or kissing whatever object had caused a breach of the rule of silence was a common practice. However it *was* optional and some novices never did it. Others, as Sister Odette said tartly, were always on their hands and knees.

These ritualized acts of mortification and self-abnegation were no more bizarre than many of the arcane customs that one can still find in the services, for example, or in any association. Their purpose was to show that the perpetrator recognized that she had disturbed the quiet of the community. The gesture showed her awareness and her contrition. These formalized acts of humility were not exhibition pieces, although I have to say that some novices made them look more than a little theatrical.

One morning Sister Mistress of Novices pulled Sister Susan and me into her office and said she felt we could benefit from some structured teaching to improve our French. "There is an excellent teacher in the infirmary called Sister Marie-Gertrude, an Irish nun who has spent most of her religious life in France. Although very crippled with arthritis, she is willing to give you two hours' tuition a week and I think it will help you."

I was pleased; my French by this time was reasonably fluent, but it was idiosyncratic.

In a small stuffy room at the top of a narrow staircase, we found our teacher. She lay immobile in bed. I was dismayed, distressed, and a little frightened by her appearance; I had never seen anybody seriously ill or indeed in pain before. I don't know what medication she was on, but it wasn't doing much for her. Below the starched bandeau and carefully arranged veil was a lined face, flushed and hectic with pain. Her little hands with their slender deformed fingers lay like broken white butterflies on the sheet. When she moved them, we could hear the little bones crackling and grinding against each other. Every movement seemed exquisite agony.

She spoke abruptly to us. I got the feeling it was taking all her effort not to cry out and consequently she didn't have much time for niceties. We went to her room twice a week for about two months, until we managed to persuade Sister Mistress of Novices that we couldn't face it any more.

She would begin each lesson with a prayer. Her voice was tremulous and angry, as if she bitterly held it against God for having visited such an affliction upon her. Right from the beginning, we had serious problems with those sessions. I don't know if she was a good teacher or not. I imagine it was her pain that made her impatient and irascible, but we never saw her smile. Our linguistic inadequacies seemed to infuriate her. She raged in particular against my handwriting. When in response to her complaints I protested defiantly that I thought my writing was stylish and elegant, she snapped, "I see nothing in it but laziness and disorder."

It was almost certainly the unattractiveness of her personality that suppressed our compassion to such an extent that shamefully we began to laugh at her. Despite many years in France, this unfortunate woman had never acquired a decent accent. This, allied to the fact that she could have done with the attention of a good dentist, meant that when she spoke French she was not always easy to understand. Her dentures rattled about in her mouth as if they had an independent life of their own. Instead of being harmoniously aligned, her upper and lower plate seemed at war with each other. They competed so fiercely for space that I always expected the vanquished one to be ejected from her mouth and to land on the open page of the grammar book, where it would sit grimly, I had no doubt, glaring up at us.

This dentine tussle for dominance was particularly noticeable at the beginning of the lesson when we recited the Lord's Prayer. Some syllables gave her more trouble than others and when she reached "Thy will be done", which in French is "*que votre volonté soit faite*", the combination of the two "vs" followed by "s" and "f" proved too much for her. The phrase became so mangled that it was as if she was attempting to articulate through a mouth filled with cotton wool while chewing on a piece of particularly sticky toffee. I prayed desperately to be delivered from this awful situation and even tried invoking the help of the Blessed Virgin, but to no avail.

One evening at recreation we were asked pleasantly if the lessons were helping. I said yes, but started to laugh and, with Sister Susan encouraging me, I began to imitate our tutor. Sister Marie-Germaine, who was in a particularly relaxed mood, laughed so loudly that Sister Mistress of Novices called us all over, exceptionally, to join the novices and I was able to give a repeat performance. Although I was reproached for being so uncharitable, they all laughed just the same. I loved being the centre of attention, but the success of this little performance was my downfall.

The next time we mounted the stairs to our class, the memory of the hilarity that I had provoked returned and, to our horror, the moment we arrived at the fatal phrase, we both began to snigger. Week by week it got worse. We could just about cope if we were alone, but together we were lost. In the end we could barely hear her open her mouth before being overcome with hilarity. Our teacher could not understand it and became increasingly furious and distressed. It must have been a mutual relief when eventually we stopped going.

Poor Sister Marie-Gertrude. We always said, Sister Susan and I, that we would go back and see her. I don't know about Sister Susan, but I never did. I was inhibited by my own bad behaviour and probably by the fear that I would start to laugh all over again. She died shortly after I returned to England; her last teaching experience had not been a happy one and we certainly contributed to that, so in retrospect I was sorry and ashamed that I hadn't made more effort to give her some pleasure among all her pain.

CHAPTER 9

House Training

About two months into our postulancy, Advent began. I loved the solemnity and the drama of this austere lead-up to Christmas. I never noticed the penitential aspect, which I thought theoretical rather than actual. Halfway through the month-long period there was a feast day, Gaudete Sunday, meaning "rejoice", a little break in the apparent severity of the period.

"Oh dear, not rillettes *and* cauliflower," groaned poor Sister Paule at supper. At tea there had been rillettes, the potted meat that I had first tasted in the little convent in Paris. This delicious dish was disastrous for those who suffered from the ubiquitous French complaint, biliousness. "*Les crises de foie*" were as common as the common cold. I laughed at the expression "a liver crisis", but for those who suffered from it, it was no laughing matter. At supper there was cauliflower, which, like all brassica, is hard to digest and considered a real no-no for those of a bilious disposition. Sister Paule was particularly susceptible and was cautious, as much as she could be, about what she ate.

"Why don't you tell Sister Mistress of Novices that this makes you ill?"

"Oh no! I can't. I'm sure we are supposed to eat whatever is put in front of us without complaining. But my tongue will be coated like felt for days, and I shall feel so heavy and sick."

"Yes, but there is a difference between just not liking something and being made ill by it." I too suffered from indigestion and I didn't complain either, but at least I didn't go yellow.

We had little choice about what we ate, although the powers that be did recognize that people could be allergic to some dishes. Sister Marie-Germaine adored both rillettes and cauliflower, and although she sometimes got away with it, more often than not, after even a mild indulgence, spent two days yellow-eyed and ashen-faced with nausea.

Recreations during this period were spent either making Christmas decorations or preparing for the winter bazaar, or "Kermesse", which took place around New Year. It was traditional for the Noviciate to hold this little sale about twice a year, at which sisters from the Mother House could buy small gifts for their families. Associated with this event, we put on a play. On this occasion, it was to be put on without costume, but on others we created amazingly successful effects, despite never removing an article of the "habit". One year we did a play about a man returning from the Crusades, who wanted to test his wife's love, so arrived home cloaked and veiled and told her he was a leper. A novice from the Irish Noviciate on her four-month stay in Evron was scandalized when she realized the novice playing the disguised husband was demanding that his wife embrace him.

"Is he asking her to kiss him?" she whispered, pink with embarrassment, giving me to understand that such a thing would never have been dreamed of in Lisdoonvarna and was certainly contrary to the spirit if not the vow of chastity.

"Actually," I replied in a whisper, "*she* is asking *her* to kiss *her*; it's a play, Sister."

At last the hero threw off his cloak and revealed himself in all the glory of his shining armour, the red cross of the crusader on his breast. The whole thing had been wonderfully created from silver foil, the chain mail from grey stockinette, the great plumed helmet from silver-painted cardboard, and turkey feathers obligingly provided by wellington-booted Sister Bernadette. A little nun from the community gasped with pleasure and exclaimed, "Heavens, how beautiful!"

It is true our audience was unsophisticated, but even so, the power of the imagination, tied to a general impression and the suspension of reality, can create remarkable illusions.

Almost everything sold at the Kermesse was made by the novices. Recreations became a sort of sewing bee and there was a preponderance of baby clothes. Nuns come in the main from Catholic families; Catholic families tend to be large, so almost everyone had relatives that included a goodly number of small children and babies. We sat at recreation like young maiden aunts, knitting matinee coats, mittens, and bonnets. Some of the more talented among us made pretty lacy dresses, the less gifted knitted scarves. We hemmed handkerchiefs; the more elaborate ones had fine drawn-thread work. Sister Odette's were exquisite. I was always surprised that someone so impulsive and quick-tempered could produce such lovely meticulous work.

"Honestly," she told me, "it's easy." She wasn't being boastful, just matter of fact. I watched her slim fingers prick the needle into the fabric and lift out the gossamer thread, then deftly pull it through.

"Yes, but you've been doing it for years." It seemed a very fiddly business. "I am more of the large canvas artist. All this dainty stuff is not for me," I told Sister Marie-Germaine, attempting to defend my pathetic efforts.

"That's a new way of describing slovenly work," she retorted sourly. She was right.

After dinner on Christmas Eve, we decorated the Noviciate. Sister Mistress of Novices came around with a huge box of chocolates, which we all accepted cheerfully. Sister Marie-Germaine hissed with disapproval.

"Advent isn't over till midnight," she commented, and although she had helped cheerfully enough with the decorations, she pointedly refused the chocolates. Sister Annie caught my eye and, when nobody was looking, took hers.

"You might have taken another for me," I said reproachfully. "I love chocolate."

"Sister Eleanor," she said, "you know that two would never be enough for you. It would make you yearn for the whole box.

I am saving you from yourself. Remember what you told me." She reminded me of the occasion when I had said that one chocolate was insufficient; if I wanted chocolates I wanted the whole lot just for me!

"Whereas, you see, two is just the right number for me!" She laughed, her enormous blue eyes sparkling. Despite her affectation, it was impossible not to like her, and she was a great giggler.

Just before Vespers Sister Mistress of Novices sent a polite note to Reverend Mother General, inviting her to come and admire the decorations. She arrived shortly after, accompanied by her councillor assistants. She too brought chocolates! Poor Sister Marie-Germaine, who normally would never have refused anything Reverend Mother General offered, was confounded. I am afraid we all smiled with malicious glee, but to be fair to her, she stuck to her guns and refused a second time with good grace.

The whole preparation for Christmas had been delightful, and quite surpassed anything I had experienced at home. My family was small: there were no uncles and aunts or jolly cousins to fill even our small house with excitement. We had a tree and put up decorations, there was turkey and Christmas pudding and gifts, but it was fairly low key compared to the anticipation and preparation in the Noviciate. I never once thought of presents.

On the top floor, high above our heads in St Cecilia, the music room, the sound of the choir practising the three Christmas Masses floated down.

"It might not be a heavenly choir," observed Sister Odette acerbically, "but it is certainly a hardworking one." We always knew if the choir practice had gone badly. Sister Marie-Suzanne would look thunderous until her normal equilibrium had been restored.

The chapel was dazzlingly bright for Midnight Mass. The traditional crib was a simple modern tableau in the Lady Chapel. On a dais two life-sized statues of the Virgin and St Joseph knelt reverently on either side of an empty manger. Mary had a particularly anxious look on her face, which I suppose given the circumstances was appropriate, but at least Joseph was young and looked as if he were capable of earning a living as a carpenter. After Mass, Reverend Mother General brought a plump and smiling baby Jesus who, judging by his size and appearance, had leapt from his mother's womb aged at least a year old and fully clothed, and laid him in the manger.

I fell asleep with the music from the Mass drumming in my ears.

The dawn Mass on Christmas Day was at 8:00 a.m., so we had a short lie-in, although it didn't amount to much as we hadn't got to bed before 1:30 a.m. There were no classes or work that day and the Office was shuffled around so all our prayers were fitted in before High Mass at 10:00 a.m. After that it was holiday. In the afternoon, wrapped up against the cold, we walked in the garden and sang carols.

Before supper we all trooped across to the refectory in the Mother House to see their tree. At first it seemed to be completely bare of decoration. Then one of the sisters went around with a lighted taper and suddenly it burst into dazzling pyrotechnic life, as the sparklers hidden in the branches flared. They only blazed for about twenty seconds, but it was one of the prettiest things I had ever seen. The tree seemed alive and dancing with thousands of effervescent silver fireflies.

"God knows what the local fire station would make of this," said Sister Susan, "but I think it's enchanting."

A few days after Christmas, Sister Marie-Germaine announced she would be going into hospital for a cataract operation. The atmosphere in the Noviciate lightened noticeably with her absence. Sister Mistress of Novices took her classes and Sister Eugenie, who was our Sewing Mistress, seized the opportunity to whisk us all up to St Anne, the sewing room. She had nine habits to make for us, as we were to be "clothed" as novices in May. Bit by bit over the following weeks, the sewing room became festooned with black dresses, cloaks, and petticoats. They hung in various stages of completion around the room like scarecrows. On the shelves, covered with cotton sheets to keep them clean, were creamy piles of white veils, chemises, linen bandeaux, and night bonnets.

Sister Eugenie's assistant, Sister Yvonne, was wicked but fun. She was an extremely competent dressmaker and very proud to say she was a tailor and not just a seamstress. Small and bandy legged, she was a dreadful gossip and sometimes pure poison dripped from her lips as her tailor's shears sliced unerringly into the reams of black cloth that she tossed onto the cutting table from the bolts we held for her. Every week she entered a competition in the local paper, convinced that one day she would win the big prize, a car. One of the novices pointed out that the Rule forbade gambling.

"Oh," she replied airily, "personal gambling is of course forbidden. I'm doing this for the community."

We found it difficult to follow the logic of this, but she was unrepentant. Sister Eugenie just smiled. The two of them sat at the old-fashioned treadle machines placed on a raised platform at the end of the room. Immaculately stitched seams rolled endlessly beneath the flashing needle. With cotton garments Sister Eugenie could open a flat seam with her horny thumbnail, and her hand sewing was exquisite. She was short on praise and would utter a brusque "good" if our work was up to scratch, but all too often she would give a disparaging little laugh, hand it back, and issue the dire directive, "It will all have to be unpicked from start to finish, my little Sister."

I loved the afternoons spent sewing. We worked in tranquil silence but took turns to read aloud. It was always something edifying, the life of a saint, sometimes a classical novel, or a biography such as *The Diary of Anne Frank*. I remember particularly a biography of the Duchess of Alençon, sister of the Empress Elizabeth of Austria. Like all the sisters in that ill-fated family she was neurotic and a hypochondriac. She was also an unfaithful wife. She became deeply religious apparently as a consequence of her contrition and made great efforts to overcome the vagaries of her temperament. She died heroically but appallingly in a fire at a charity bazaar, refusing to leave the building until all her helpers were safe and so died trapped in the stairwell. She was identified by the remains of her hip-length golden-red hair. Despite her courage

I thought she sounded a dreary woman and much preferred the feisty Anne.

The queue outside the Noviciate for the sale on New Year's Day was impressive. The community began arriving in ones and twos after dinner and by 1:30 p.m. stretched all the way back under the covered way to the door of the Mother House. Some of the fitter sisters had even come down from the infirmary. Sister Marie-Suzanne stood like the Harrods doorman preventing anyone from jumping the gun, but when on the stroke of 2:30 p.m. she opened the door, she was swept aside in the rush. A tide of black and white surged down the passage. Everyone had been given a small amount of money. Nuns in those days handled no money of their own, so this was quite an exciting event. I don't think I have ever seen such determined shoppers. Each time we had a sale the goods were virtually the same, so although there had been no preview, everybody knew what to expect. The only unexpected items were on the bric-a-brac stall. These had been donated by friendly shopkeepers in town: useless and usually ugly little china ornaments, tray cloths and writing paper, coloured pencils, plant holders, glass vases, and, unexpectedly, a nice leather purse. Goods were picked up, examined, and tossed aside. We had to be strict.

"Sister, I can't sell you seven calendars. There won't be enough for anybody else!"

"Well how many *can* I have?"

"Two. I can let you have two."

"Two – *two*? But I have six nieces and my aunt always gets a calendar. What can I give them?"

"Something else, Sister." Poor Sister Susan was harassed.

We had to keep a sharp eye on one or two. Sister Pauline from the infirmary, whose dementia was harmless and engaging, was a skilful shoplifter. Reverend Mother General took her kindly in charge, removing things gently from her as swiftly as she purloined them. She went away an hour or so later, happy with honest purchases.

The whole thing was an exercise in innocent consumerism. I saw only excited, happy, and satisfied customers, light years away from the frenetic shopping that characterizes so much bargain-hunting at sale times today.

Sister Marie-Germaine's absence was a relief for me. I had begun quite foolishly to demonize her. During recreation I also complained vociferously about her to anybody prepared to listen. I was too silly and self-obsessed to notice that my companions, although sympathetic, were a little embarrassed by my outbursts. They too suffered from the unpredictability of our Postulant Mistress, but their sense of propriety, which clearly I lacked, moderated their own comments.

Eventually my "Guardian Angel", Sister Jeanne, took pity on me and suggested that I go and talk to Sister Mistress of Novices. So I asked to see her.

In her light airy office she listened to me in silence as I poured out my grievances: "She is so inconsistent and she brings out the worst in me."

When I had finished and my voice trailed off lamely, she sat for a moment and I sat looking at her. Then she spoke briefly, but slowly and carefully, making sure I understood every word. Looking out of the window and in a detached voice without the slightest hint of complicity, she said, "I know Sister Marie-Germaine can be difficult, but she has been placed here by a legitimate Superior who recognizes her qualities. She has a lot to teach you and you have a lot to learn from her."

She responded vehemently to my sceptical sigh. "It is your duty to take direction from her; she knows more than you do about the religious life. In any event, you have a responsibility to love her and help her to see Christ's presence in you and in herself. Do you think she too isn't struggling on the path to perfection? See it as a challenge, part of the pattern that God has laid down for you."

She thought for a moment, then went on slowly, "Your religious life, wherever you are, does not fundamentally have anything to do with Sister Marie-Germaine or Sister Marie-Suzanne or me or indeed any Sister Superior you will have in the future. Your life, your relationship, is with God. This congregation, our Rule, even the companions that surround you, are only the framework within which you find him. The real relationship is intimate, is personal. You must make room for him here," she touched my forehead, "but above all here." Smiling, she touched my breast lightly. "It's only with the heart that one understands." She laughed. "I'm afraid that's not original. You must read *The Little Prince* by Antoine de Saint-Exupéry: you'll enjoy it."

She was not a particularly handsome woman, too loose-limbed so that she often seemed a bit clumsy. Fair-skinned and heavy-featured, a little jowly, her ice-blue myopic eyes shielded by thick glasses, her only beauty was lovely hands, with long, fine, square-ended fingers. In repose she was calm, elegant, even statuesque, and she had a presence, a spirit, a manner so her own, so compelling, that I was mesmerized by her. I wondered how this had escaped me all the time I had been under the same roof. Instead of turning to her for help, I had been overwhelmed by petty irritations, more to do with my own self-esteem than with reality.

As I got to know her better I would see, little by little, her own defects, which were clearly evident: her tendency toward favouritism; her occasional thoughtless use of wit, which alarmed and sometimes hurt the less self-assured; her little self-indulgences; her flashes of sarcasm. But she was so warmly human, so shot through with the wonderful combination of virtues and flaws, that despite it all, for me she seemed to be the perfect role model. I thought a lot about that interview. Was this what a vocation was all about? Not just being called to serve and to love in a general kind of way but to enter into a close, intimate, unique relationship with God? The reality of it and its implications began, just began, to come home to me.

I was determined to try very hard with Sister Marie-Germaine after that and would like to say that our relationship improved, but if anything, on her return, her awareness that I had fallen under the influence of someone she disliked, resented, and mistrusted only made things worse. We struggled on together through the remaining few months of my postulancy with a greater or lesser degree of success. As my French improved, so interaction with her became easier, but not necessarily more affable. She could still be gratuitously unpleasant and then unexpectedly kind. It was of course her inconsistency that made her so irritating.

Although my time in the Noviciate as a postulant had not been all plain sailing, as the longed-for date of the "clothing" approached I began to feel more confident and less apprehensive about the possibility of being sent home, if not in disgrace, at least as having been found wanting. I felt settled and secure, and consequently a good deal of my need for frenetic activity calmed down. I did at last begin to believe I was hearing God's voice in the lovely community prayer. The Office began to have real meaning and spoke to me in an intimate and immediate sort of way.

At the beginning of May we all made official application to be admitted to the congregation as novices. It was all very formal this time. The letter to the Reverend Mother General was personal but stylized, in that it followed a specific format. I found this odd, as it seemed so stilted.

"Why can't I just write my own letter?" I wanted to know.

"Listen to me," sighed Sister Marie-Germaine. "Reverend Mother General is a busy woman. She has nine of your letters, eight from second-year novices, heaven knows how many others from sisters applying to renew temporal vows, and certainly some applying for final vows. Do you think she's going to lie in bed till three o'clock in the morning reading your purple prose? She wants to skim through them, see they are all in order, and then send them to the bishop for his approval. It's both quicker and easier if they are all in the same format. It's like filling in a form. A very important one, of course," she added quickly.

So my application was accepted and I was told that I would be admitted to the congregation as a novice. Sister Marie-Germaine embraced us all warmly and with genuine pleasure at our admission. Our last evening as postulants was one of the pleasantest recreations we ever spent with her.

Many of us were bold enough to tell her about episodes of which we thought she had been ignorant: the extra chocolates Sister Annie had pilfered, which she said she *had* noticed, and my reading of Damon Runyon; Sister Odette confessing to scooping all her veal stew into her hankie because she so hated the taste and was sure she'd never keep it down.

"What did you do with it?" we all asked.

"I kept it in my pocket till recreation, then put it down the lavatory!"

Then Sister Annie decided to join in this fit of the honesties. "We need to tell you something, Sister." She nodded to include me, and I wondered with apprehension what was about to be disclosed.

"You know your cheese plants – the ones we had to move from the Noviciate into the cloister because they grew so tall, like Jack's beanstalk? They were such a nightmare to clean, all those holey leaves, we got a bit bored, and Sister Eleanor had been teaching us the songs from a musical play in London."

She looked to me for confirmation. I nodded. "Yes, *My Fair Lady*."

I remembered the episode that she was about to reveal only too well. I had begun to hum and then, emboldened by the empty cloister, with my duster suspended from my fingers like Pavarotti, began to sashay toward Sister Annie, singing louder and louder. My companion, nothing loath, entered into the spirit of the thing and began also to sashay toward me. When we met in the middle, it seemed the most natural thing to dance.

We had got all the way to the chapel and were halfway back up the cloister again. I had reached "I could have danced, danced, danced all night" and was just executing quite a creditable reverse turn, so that my back was toward the chapel door, when it opened soundlessly. Sister Annie's horrified face had alerted me to the situation.

At this point in her tale, I risked a glance at Sister Marie-Germaine. Leaning forward, she enquired, "And?"

"Well," I said, taking over from Sister Annie, "we were frozen with horror. There's a game called musical statues, where nobody moves. It was a bit like that. Then Reverend Mother began to pace toward us – you know how stately she is – and we fled from her, desperately trying to gather up mops and buckets and dusters, and making a terrible racket, and dropping things and having to go back for stuff."

I noticed that our Postulant Mistress, by this stage, had begun to laugh.

"Reverend Mother didn't laugh," said Sister Annie. "When she reached us, she began to make these odd shooing movements, as if she was herding geese, and then she just swept past, went out the end of the cloister, and disappeared into her study."

"I expect she thought she was – herding geese, I mean. I imagine she was wondering what on earth to say to you, as I don't suppose she had the slightest idea what you were doing."

This turned out to be true, as I learned much later on. By this stage, Sister Marie-Germaine, almost helpless with laughter, had her handkerchief out and was mopping her eyes.

"Didn't she tell you?" I asked. "Oh, surely she must have done."

"Not a word. She knew I'd laugh; look at me now. I expect she relied on Sister Mistress of Novices to scold you."

She was correct. We had both faced a cool reprimand and a reminder that the cloister was a place where silence should be maintained as strictly as possible. Singing and dancing of the kind we were indulging in was inappropriate. Sister Annie's rash observation that we were in good company, as King David had danced, and naked at that, as the ark of the covenant was being brought to Jerusalem, elicited the riposte that King David was King David and that she, Annie, was Annie, and that she had better not consider dancing, naked or otherwise, anywhere within the convent precincts, or she would find herself dancing all the way back to Versailles.

PART 2

Noviciate

CHAPTER 10

"Taking the Veil"

We had a five-day retreat before our "clothing", and I loved this quiet and reflective time. The weather was beautiful, mild and sunny and, apart from Mass, the Office, and the twice daily conferences, we were allowed free rein to come and go as we pleased. Walking down the avenues, I found myself thinking vaguely of friends left behind. It all seemed very remote and so detached from my present life. I was busy and learning so many new things, increasingly convinced that I was in the right place and that God was drawing me to an as yet uncertain but intriguing new way of life. It was still an adventure and, I was beginning to feel, a romantic one at that.

The rite of passage that marks the official entry into the congregation as a novice is traditionally a public event. The contrast between the first part of the ceremony, with its procession of young women in bridal dresses, and the second, when the novices return clothed in the severity of their habits, always elicits a gasp, probably of admiration, possibly of dismay.

We put on our white dresses in Sister Mistress of Novices' anteroom and sat on chairs placed around the walls, like girls at a village dance waiting for a partner. A sister came to take photographs. In the mirror I caught sight of myself. I looked serious and dumpy, not unlike Queen Victoria, all short neck and pouter pigeon bosom. The style was very fifties, so even in 1962 it looked old fashioned. On our heads we wore "Juliet caps" with shoulder-length veils of white tulle; on our feet, white stockings and white pumps. The dress was lovely on the tall and slim but it certainly did me no favours!

The procession took us from the Noviciate through the Great Corridor in the Mother House to the large oak double doors leading into the basilica. Sister Mistress of Novices preceded us and we were followed by Reverend Mother General, her councillors and by the rest of the community in serried ranks. The Great Corridor was lined with children from local schools and colleges. Their whispering hushed as we passed between them, our dresses whispering back as they fell silent. As we entered the basilica, I saw the choir, their eyes undoubtedly fixed on the raised hands of Sister Marie-Suzanne, waiting for our entrance before she drew out from them the exultingly sweet notes of the Magnificat. It floated upwards, across the heads turned expectantly toward us. Halfway down the nave I saw my parents. My father caught my eye and gave me the most enormous wink. He looked unimaginably proud.

On a low table in front of the altar lay nine neat, folded piles, black habits, white veils, and waiting for us was the bishop, magnificently mitred and crosiered. In the cavernous space of the church, our voices, even in unison, were thin and reedy as we made our request to be received as novices.

Our folded habits with the creamy novice veil on top were placed on our outstretched arms; it seemed a wonderful moment. The choir sang on blissfully. I felt overwhelmed with joy and moved in a daze of happiness. As we went back down the nave to the Mother House to be clothed, the Te Deum burst out and rolled behind us down the Great Corridor as far as the Chapter Room.

Reverend Mother General, her councillor assistants, and all the sisters from the Noviciate were waiting for us. Our bridal dresses were stripped from us with a minimum of care. They lay strewn in great white pools on the polished parquet, like camellias that had dropped from the tree and begun to go a little brown at the edges. The veils and Juliet caps were tossed aside over the kneelers so that immediately the place took on the air of a jaded bedroom strewn with party clothes, abandoned by owners too tired to put them away. They were gathered up and bundled away to be cleaned later and then hung up in sheets packed with lavender for the following year.

Under our white dresses, in preparation for the "habit", we wore a curious garment called a "chemise": a long-sleeved, round-necked garment like an eighteenth-century shift. Over this went a black waist petticoat with pockets. We pulled on black stockings and black shoes. Behind us Sister Mistress of Novices and Sister Marie-Germaine twisted our hair back into a knot and pinned it firmly in place. I had a momentary mental picture of Audrey Hepburn's hair being brutally shorn in *The Nun's Story* and was pleased we were not being subjected to such indignity.

Sister Mistress of Novices' hands were gentle on either side of my face as she pulled on the bandeau covering my head and brow, tightened the drawstring, and tied it firmly. The habit was slipped over my head, adjusted, and done up, the narrow inner sleeves were fastened, and the wide outer sleeves folded back with an inverted pleat. We waited in turn to have our veils smoothed over our heads, kneeling and kissing them before they were placed in position, and then pinning them behind our ears. Reverend Mother General blessed us all; we took lighted candles, formed up in line, and began the return journey to the basilica. The whole event, effecting a complete transformation of our appearance, took no more than twenty minutes.

We knelt during the long singing of the Litany of the Saints. There was no full-length prostration, although, as my back began to ache from five minutes of unsupported kneeling, I would have been quite pleased to have lain face down! The bishop's homily was short and to the point. He spoke about the meaning of the religious life and its value and importance to the church as a "powerhouse of prayer". He spoke about sacrifice and glory, about following in Christ's footsteps, and what an honour it was for us to have been given the grace of a vocation.

Afterwards we gathered with our families on the terrace and

the bishop, accompanied by Reverend Mother General, circulated politely. He became deeply engrossed in conversation with my mother, who spoke a little French. He had worked in Glasgow in his youth and was polite enough to say his memories of the city were "rich and interesting". I hadn't seen my parents for nearly eight months and was desperately anxious to get rid of him so that I could have them to myself. I knew our time together was limited. The previous afternoon I had spent in restless anticipation of my parents' arrival. Finally Sister Eugenie took pity on me and carted me off to St Anne to help put the final touches to the pile of new habits and veils for the next day.

"Don't muddle them up, whatever you do," she stressed. "One year we had a terrible mix-up and spent an infernal time re-sorting them, dresses coming off and on, everybody waiting and His Grace wondering what the hold-up was. Not a man to be kept waiting, our bishop."

This flustered me a little and I had a mental picture of tall and slender Sister Susan struggling to fit into a habit made for sturdy Sister Eleanor. I was so apprehensive that momentarily I forgot about my family's arrival, so when Sister Mistress of Novices put her head around the door to say with a smile, "They're here," it took a second or two to think what she meant.

I shot down the stairs, raced through the covered way, and rocketed into the Great Corridor, pulling up sharply outside Reverend Mother General's office before taking off again, once clear of her door. One never liked to be caught rushing anywhere by that stately lady.

My relationship with my father had often been stormy, but on this occasion our meeting, as we hugged and kissed, was one of unalloyed pleasure. My mother looked thin and, although I didn't know it at the time, was already beginning to suffer from the effects of an addiction to prescribed amphetamines that would ravage her middle age.

Once the bishop had finally moved on we escaped into the gardens, where we spent the remains of the afternoon and evening strolling up and down the avenues of hornbeam. I knew it would be a year before I saw my parents again.

We were together for a short time after supper, then said our goodbyes, my mother in tears. I left them blithely. Walking slowly back through the Great Corridor to the Noviciate, I felt nothing but pleasure that they had been able to come, and relief that they had gone and I could at long last "get started".

The beginning of the noviciate, for the congregation and for the novice herself, marks a sea change. She hasn't taken vows but she lives as if she has, so there is, during the two years of the noviciate, a process not only of instruction and learning, but also one of application. She practises what are known as the three evangelical counsels: poverty, chastity, and obedience; the recommendation given by Christ to the young man who asked what he must do to become perfect after having followed all the Commandments and the laws. Jesus said, "If you wish to be perfect, go and sell what you own and give the money to the poor [poverty]... then come, follow me [obedience and chastity]" (Matthew 19:21). Her daily life, like that of the professed religious, is governed by the "Rule".

The first year of the period of the noviciate in the Congregation of the Sisters of Evron was called the canonical year and, with rare exceptions, had to be completed in its entirety. Nobody must be able to offer as an excuse "I didn't know what I was letting myself in for", or "I wasn't there the day they did the lesson on the vows". The length of time that a novice could be absent from the physical building of the Noviciate without invalidating her canonical year was clearly defined. Occasionally, a novice had to leave the confines of the building. Sister Paule, for example, went home to see her dying mother and subsequently returned home a second time for the funeral. In such circumstances it was up to the bishop of the diocese to decide whether the whole canonical year had to be repeated, the elapsed time that a novice was absent made up, or whether the absence could be excused. In all cases he would count on the recommendations of the Reverend Mother

General and her Council, who would have consulted the Sister Mistress of Novices.

Although the noviciate was both a period of time and a physical place, the Noviciate Reverend Mother General and the Council could authorize the relocation of the latter so that when we went on holiday en masse, as we did for a fortnight each year, the building in which we stayed became de facto the Noviciate and the Canonical Year was maintained in its integrity.

This was a year of spiritual training. First-year novices could not teach, nurse, or participate in any of the charitable activities of the congregation; they were under "formation". They had very limited access to books or literature of any kind other than those of a strictly religious nature; and there was no more Damon Runyon.

I had expected my new costume, the "habit", to feel cumbersome and hot, so was agreeably surprised by how much more comfortable it was to wear than the ungainly and inelegant postulant's uniform. The whole ritual associated with the wearing of the habit was as formal and as stylized as any military uniform. The Rule specified everything, down to the minutest detail of style, material, and manner: the width of the pleats, the height of the hem from the ground and its depth, the lengths of the sleeves, their width, how far down the hand they came (to the fingertips). Nothing was haphazard.

We had to take great care of our habit, as we only had the one. The skirt tended to get shiny at the seat and the pleats suffered. To minimize fraying, the underside of the hem had a sort of braid, sewn along the inferior edge. Despite this, the lower part of the skirt tended to suffer a degree of wear and tear. There were some actions that could be taken to minimize the damage, such as holding it up outside in bad weather, always pinning up the skirt for housework, wearing an apron, and picking it up when going up and down stairs. I have been watching costume dramas for forty years and have only once seen a long skirt being dealt with correctly. All these heroines tripping daintily downstairs are all so obviously modern women who have never had to deal with a long dress as part of everyday wear. Going upstairs, you pick up the *front*, but coming downstairs you pick up the *back* of the dress. Failure to do so means, first, that you risk catching your heel in the skirt as it trails behind you and, secondly, you'll be through the hem inside three months. After a short time, this care became automatic, although for the first week or so "your skirt, your skirt" sounded through the house like a sort of mantra, until we began to get the hang of it.

Summers in central France are considerably warmer than in England and I did find it hot at first, but the body adapts very quickly. I was much more concerned about the problem of perspiration and the likelihood of BO. The whole problem of underwear was a nightmare. The chemise was changed once a week and doubled up as a nightdress, so it was next to my skin constantly for seven days. Initially I found this repellent but, as I found out, one can get used to almost anything and there were other things that I found worse. Our other underwear and stockings were also changed on a weekly basis. I didn't mind too much about my bra but was horrified at the thought of wearing knickers, particularly interlock ones, for that length of time. Eventually, after some weeks, the underwear issue was resolved and we were more or less given the freedom to change our pants when we wished, although Sister Eugenie, who was in charge of the laundry, muttered about the excessive washing: it would wear out the clothes and was clearly against the spirit if not the vow of poverty.

I had to hope that my own hygiene, the bidet where I washed more than my feet, and the concessionary weekly bath would be sufficient to deal with any personal problems. I was never aware of my companions being unsavoury, nor indeed myself. However, on my eventual return to England I discovered that dear Mother Henrietta, Provincial Superior, provided basic roll-on deodorants in the general store cupboard of "things in common" and she directed me pointedly toward it, so I have to assume that I was more malodorous than I had supposed.

There were other aspects of these personal constraints that I did find difficult. I hated my hairy legs and hairier armpits, even though they were only seen by me. I never conquered this small intimate vanity.

I did have a problem with skin cracking behind my ears. The constrictions of the bandeau meant that the area behind the ear got sweaty and sore, and then would become raw. This was exacerbated by wearing a night bonnet. It tied under the chin and, although quite plain and without any frill, was appealing to look at, but it was very uncomfortable and almost never stayed on. I invariably woke with the wretched thing around my neck or on the floor because one of the ribbons had snapped. At bedtime, in our white chemises, with our brown faces and hands, white foreheads and rim of hair under the archaic bonnets, we looked like Siamese cats.

The departure of the second-year novices left space for us both in the dormitory and at the novices' table. I was disappointed that Sister Mistress of Novices was no less heavy-handed with the serving spoon. We all continued to receive what seemed to my eyes to be enormous portions of everything. We ate extremely well; I just found it all too much. Because the noviciate was stressful, weight loss was common and more to be feared than weight gain, because of the association with anorexia. Getting fatter was therefore viewed as a good thing. We were always being told, "*Une âme saine dans un corps sain*" (A healthy soul in a healthy body). It was extraordinary that some novices, despite being virtually force fed, actually got thinner. Night after night I lay in bed, my stomach uncomfortably distended. It was the start of digestive problems from which I have suffered all my life since.

CHAPTER 11

A Novice's Life for Me!

The move from the postulants' classroom to Sacré-Coeur was for me one of unadulterated relief and pleasure. I was in awe of Sister Marie-Suzanne, our Choir Mistress, Mistress of Studies, and Deputy Novice Mistress, who now had day-to-day charge of us. She turned out to be delightful, intelligent, warm-hearted, and sweet-natured, with a dry sense of humour. She was deeply devout and had a kind of glowing spirituality. Although a strict disciplinarian she was a wonderful example to us, as she was, above all, a model of calmness and order.

Our daily life as novices was busy. The rising bell was at 5:30 a.m. I quite liked the early start: in fact one of the elements that most appealed to me about the religious life was its asceticism. I liked the ritual, the choreography, and solemnity of the Office; the chanting, the purity, and stylistic melody of the Gregorian plainchant.

The first waking sound after the bell was Sister Marie-Suzanne's voice: "Praise the Sacred Heart of Jesus." To which we replied, often sleepily, "Praise the Immaculate Heart of Mary."

We got up immediately; there was no turning over and snatching a few more minutes. We were due in chapel at 6:00 a.m. There was one small mirror for all of us, to ensure our veils were on straight, and then it was downstairs to our rank to wait for the second bell. Any latecomers would have to slip sheepishly into their place after the rest of the sisters had filed into chapel. I loved the few brief steps along the covered way to the Mother House. If it was raining, the lights turned water dripping from the gutter into a falling sheet of flame, and in the milky, pale blue summer mornings the world felt fresh and new.

The first Office of the day was Laudes, chanted on a single note; if the tone dropped and flattened, our Choir Mistress blew it again on a tiny silver mouth organ, sometimes irately, whereupon the entire community responded with a sort of musical swoop upwards, the opposite of a nose-dive.

This was followed by half an hour of meditation. We no longer had Sister Marie-Germaine's serene direction; we were on our own. Occasionally I nodded off, but we all contrived to keep each other awake, so a gentle or vigorous dig in the ribs was usually enough. It was harder in the winter. The central heating was minimal and when it was very cold we were given permission to wear our cloaks, which were normally outdoor dress. Having those wrapped around us did not predispose to wakefulness.

Mass was at 6:45 a.m. and this was followed by the Office of Prime. By the time we had breakfast at 7:30 a.m., we had been at prayer for an hour and a half. We had barely twenty minutes for breakfast. Prayer and work formed part of the ethos of the congregation, so as soon as we had finished eating, we turned up our skirts, put on our blue aprons, rolled back our sleeves and did the housework. This was no trivial event; we are not talking about a quick go around with a vacuum cleaner and a flick of a duster. The Noviciate was a series of long corridors and large rooms, and some of them, including the refectory, dormitories, and Sacré-Coeur, were very large indeed. The refectory floor had unglazed tiles, rather attractive but extraordinarily difficult to clean. The floor was uneven and the tiles sweated, so that every two or three days a soft, damp, and fluffy line of mould would appear around the edges. This had to be scrubbed away with a sort of flat brush, which was attached to one's shoe by a broad strap. It was excellent exercise. The free foot shuffled forward and the foot with the attachment scrubbed, but it took a good twenty minutes with two of us working to remove the mould. Then the floor had to be swept and washed.

"If we were to put less water on the floor, the tiles wouldn't get so damp," Sister Paule said to me at evening recreation. "They are very porous."

"It's no good asking me. I've never in my life cleaned anything like that. At home we have carpets."

"What, in the dining room?" She was clearly astonished.

"Well, yes, actually." It was difficult to explain that the whole process, both of serving food and eating it, was so different in England. "We don't get crumbs on the floor much. We don't eat the same sort of bread, we hardly ever have soup, and the vegetables are cooked in water. There's no oil or butter on anything, except butter on toast. I never tasted vinaigrette till I came here. Oily things hardly ever get spilled because we don't have oily things."

"No vinaigrette! What do you put on salad?" No vinaigrette was clearly unimaginable.

"There is a sort of sauce in a bottle called salad cream. It's quite nice actually." I began to feel apologetic. Cleaning, cooking: we were obviously, as a nation, not up to scratch at all.

"You must have tiles in the kitchen?" She was intrigued and clearly not going to let this one drop.

"No, we have something called lino... It's made of... well, I don't know what it's made of, but we don't have to scrub it." I thought it was time to distract her. "What are we going to do with all those grease spots tomorrow?"

Sometimes the marks were so numerous that the entire floor had to be scrubbed with soda, not just washed. The doors leading out onto a veranda would be opened and great buckets of water thrown down to rinse the soda off and then chased down the steps outside. On one occasion two novices soaked the convent chaplain who happened to be passing. He took it in very good part but it convulsed us all when, at the Chapter of Faults a week later, they both accused themselves of "careless impetuosity with a bucket of water".

Dusting was taken seriously too. The whole process of housework was imbued with a spiritual significance over and above its practical necessity. It was part of everyday living but was also an exercise in asceticism. There was never any effort made to render it more efficient, to save time, or to make it easier for us. The beautiful parquet floors were polished with a weighted "bumper". A dust pan and brush were things found in even the humblest of homes; in the Noviciate we had dust pans, but a goose wing replaced a small brush and while this was ideal for getting into corners, it was less than effective for generally collecting the little piles of dirt. Poor Sister Susan with her feather phobia turned pale when she saw this archaic cleaning implement. She was excused from that particular aspect of housework but not from the equally archaic system for cleaning the toilet bowls.

One bright morning I saw that Sister Paule and I were detailed to clean Sacré-Coeur for the week. This also, I was informed, included the five outdoor lavatory cubicles in the little courtyard that abutted the Noviciate.

"Have you ever cleaned lavatory pans?" asked Sister Paule.

I was surprised by the question and a little puzzled. "Yes, of course. It's not difficult. You put cleaner or bleach down and then scrub away with the lavatory brush."

She didn't answer, disappeared out of the courtyard, and reappeared a moment or two later with a bucket and two enormous floor cloths. Under my horrified gaze, she stuffed the first cloth into the loo and by means of several vigorous thrusts shunted the water out of sight and presumably around the U-bend. She pulled out the cloth and wrung it out into the bucket, then sprinkled the empty pan with some scouring powder and proceeded to scrub it. It did look very clean. When it was done, she flushed the loo with an air of triumph and then, looking sceptically at me, enquired if I felt up to doing the next one. I definitely felt a gauntlet was being thrown down and although I would have preferred a pair of rubber gloves, I assured her that of course I could manage it, although at one point I felt my gorge rise when I thought of... when I thought of what I was doing, and to this day I think it was both unnecessary and singularly unhygienic.

Under her breath, and in English for my benefit, Sister Susan, among the others watching this performance, murmured, "It's clearly a 'black pudding' moment."

Sister Annie looked equally appalled. Swallowing hard she announced bravely that *she* could cope with anything.

"I didn't say I couldn't cope with it," reposted Sister Susan tartly. "I just think it shows an elementary failure to understand the purpose of a U-bend." As far as I can remember, she and I undertook this unpleasant and repellent job with as much determination and efficiency as our French companions.

The day-to-day housework finished just before 9:00 a.m., when the bell rang and we removed our aprons and took our place in Sacré-Coeur for the Office of Tierce, which took about five minutes. A range of different study periods filled the rest of the morning.

Bible study was taken by Sister Marie-Suzanne. Her classes were a revelation to me. Brought up as an English Roman Catholic, I was pitifully ignorant of the richness contained in the Old Testament. It was the spiritual aspect rather than the dubious historical data that our teacher was concerned with; nevertheless she brought those charismatic characters and wickedly fascinating kings to wonderful life. David, the golden boy, dazzling in his bravado; it was always clear, I thought, that poor bumbling Goliath didn't stand a chance against such a lithe and nimble opponent. Then there was gorgeous, sexy Solomon, something of a megalomaniac with his vast building programmes, and his even vaster harems. What attractive, glamorous people they were, with their loyalties, betrayals, sorrows, lusts, and loves. Those fearsome, bloodthirsty, demagogic warrior judges; I half-expected to see them leap off the pages and tear along the flat desktop toward me, brandishing swords, their hair and beards on fire with divine retribution.

Then there were the gentle Minor Prophets – Hosea was one of Sister Marie-Suzanne's special favourites. The monumental foursome of Isaiah, Daniel, Ezekiel, and Jeremiah was as real to her as we, her novices, were. She loved the Song of Songs and we listened to her with awe as she read aloud that great sensual poem of physical passion with such purity of intent and such tenderness that we were utterly convinced by her declaration that this was the perfect imagery of God's love for us. For two years I listened to her speak of God's plan for his people, both of the Old and New Diaspora, and have never found anyone who could match her.

She was not as compelling on church history. Her view that the church was beyond reproach was justified by her conviction that one had to separate the agents from the spiritual entity: bad priests didn't make a bad church any more than bad husbands invalidated marriage. I was happy with that, but didn't think it put the agents themselves beyond criticism.

"What about Alexander Borgia?" I once asked. "And Boniface VIII? They were monstrous."

"They were popes," she replied firmly. "Do you think the Holy Ghost didn't know what he was doing? Are you challenging the wisdom of God? Do we fully understand his plan?"

"What about Galileo? The church was wrong about Galileo."

Sister Marie-Suzanne drew her breath in sharply. "No," she asserted firmly, "the church was not wrong about Galileo. He was a man ahead of his time. The church has a responsibility toward all its members. Maybe it would have done great harm to have encouraged him at a time when most people would have been terrified of such radical ideas."

She was obdurate; the church had been misrepresented, misunderstood. The Inquisition, on which I must say she didn't dwell over much, took place, she asserted, at a time when tolerance, particularly religious tolerance, was a foreign concept. Of course it wouldn't be justifiable today, but *autres temps autres mœurs* (other times, other morals or standards).

It was the same with her classes on the history of our congregation. The book from which she drew her information was sycophantic in the extreme. It was based almost entirely on the reigns of the various Reverend Mother Generals, all of whom had been virtuous beyond belief. Not one was incompetent, ineffectual, average, or even just ordinary. They were all "remarkable", even "extraordinary".

What was so strange about this lack of impartial critical analysis was that she was perfectly ready to accept all the faults and failings of her biblical heroes and heroines. She was highly critical of the incestuous coupling of Lot with his daughters, and of David sending Uriah to the front line so he could sleep with Bathsheba. She deplored Ruth's behaviour, crawling brazenly into Boaz's bed, selling herself for a better life, with her mother-in-law virtually pimping for her. Even God came in for some reproach. He had been overly harsh on Moses, she thought, denying him the Promised Land because of one transgression, after he had so faithfully shepherded the Israelites toward their goal.

Her lack of critical analysis of the church and the congregation was puzzling. I can only think that she shied away from it because she feared it might be misinterpreted. The Rule was firm on this: challenging received wisdom was indicative of "a critical spirit" and this was reprehensible. I didn't mind too much about the past Reverend Mother Generals, but I was and still am more than a little uneasy about the whitewash that the church applies to all those "difficult periods".

CHAPTER 12

So Much to Learn, to Love, and to Understand

All the lectures relating to the religious life were given by Sister Mistress of Novices. They were serious, and our conversation at our twice daily recreation period was immeasurably enlivened as we discussed and debated them. It was clear that community life involved tolerance and mutual support, but it was also to do with seeking and finding God living among us and helping others to find him. I realized that I had to take a long hard look at my irritation and impatience with some of my sister novices, not to mention my attitude to Sister Marie-Germaine!

Sister Mistress of Novices' lectures made the religious life sound such an adventure, a leap into the unknown. We were called, she insisted, not to an unnatural but to a supernatural life. The vows were nothing in themselves – sterile, futile, and restrictive – but lived in the light of an ongoing permanent offering to God and a chosen path following Christ, they became luminous. We must live like St Paul, as if we could already "see the invisible", and because of that simple little sentence, I was more tolerant of Paul's radical misogyny, seeing it as more understandable in the light of the culture of the time. To live as if the invisible were tangible, to feel the hand of God, to know his love, seemed to me the ultimate joy. I didn't think it any less true because the lecturer was such a seductive speaker, and I recognized the element of high emotion that her lectures generated.

"This business of the *virtue* of poverty, chastity, and obedience is all new to me," confided Sister Odette at evening recreation. We were sitting, as usual, in a circle, our hands supposedly busy with knitting and sewing. In the evening, summer or winter, recreation was inside. There was always a lot of mending to be done and if we had none of our own, Sister Eugenie could always be relied on to find some for us. Like Homer's faithful Penelope, we sometimes unravelled the knitting of the previous day in order to avoid hemming unidentifiable articles for the sewing room. I think we imagined we were not within earshot of either Sister Mistress of Novices or Sister Marie-Germaine. The evening sun, low in the sky, reflected off the parquet and lent Sacré-Coeur an unexpected cosiness. There was a pleasant buzz of conversation; we were a relaxed little group.

"I suppose it means that you can take the vows," Sister Odette continued, rethreading her needle, "and yet in many ways not be practising the application of them."

We were all momentarily silent as we digested this thought, but she was quite right. It is perfectly possible to live without infringing the vows and yet never be living the spirit of them.

There are two main elements to the vows: the vow itself and the virtue, the daily practice of the vow. A nun can only default against the vow of obedience if she refuses to do something asked of her *in the name of that vow*. Obedience is weighty, because it directs and encapsulates not only the other two vows but the whole of the religious life. Asking a nun to do something in the name of her vow of obedience is done extremely rarely, with "prudence and precaution", and should be done in writing and in the presence of two witnesses; so said our Rule. When a nun is sent from one convent to take up a post in another, this is called "receiving her obedience". For most, if they have been happy and fulfilled in a particular convent, they will receive their new posting with some regret. They may protest, even vociferously, but they will eventually accept the move, albeit with some sadness. The obstinate refusal by a nun to move would be considered a serious matter and in some circumstances might constitute a fault against the vow.

"Yes," sighed Sister Paule, "but it's the virtue that is so hard. To obey as the Rule says, *promptly, wholeheartedly, disinterestedly, cheerfully, and generously,* particularly if your Sister Superior is someone you don't like or admire, that's difficult!"

I looked at her round, pleasant face and wondered. She always appeared to me a stunning example of someone who seemed completely at home in convent life. Later she told me that coming from a country background, the constraints of the noviciate lifestyle were often almost unbearable.

"And what about judgment?" interjected Sister Odette again, moving her stool to get better light for her sewing. She was obviously wrestling with this, judging by her furrowed brow and air of concentration. I was always impressed that she could produce such intricate work and yet continue an in-depth conversation. "We are expected to be cooperative and to submit our will and even our judgment to a Superior in all reasonable requests. Supposing we don't trust her judgment? What is a *reasonable request*? What," she continued, "if your Superior is ill-informed or unstable? Obedience would become a real burden and a daily grind."

In the silence that followed we heard Sister Mistress of Novices' calm voice. "It is always best to have the mindset of obedience. How can one know if another's judgment is better or worse than one's own? If there is serious doubt, or if you thought a request or command were dangerous, you have recourse to the Provincial Superior or Reverend Mother General."

"That's all very well, but suppose the demand *came* from the Provincial Superior or Reverend Mother General herself? What then? Run to the bishop?" Sister Odette looked around and got a general murmur of agreement.

"How absolute you all are," sighed Sister Mistress of Novices. "If we get a demand from a Provincial Superior or from Reverend Mother General herself, then we must assume that the request is being made in the name of the vow, and then the usual safeguards apply."

Poverty seemed easier to deal with. A nun gives up all the management of any goods and property she might possess or inherit. She can't keep any money that she earns nor any material gift that she might be given. Usually, over a period of time, nuns do acquire things, little presents, but these are always ephemeral. In practice, of course, a kind and understanding Superior would be indulgent and let nuns take things with them, but it was by no means automatic. It meant, if the letter of the Rule was observed, that you never accumulated anything. You always had the same number of garments when you left a convent to go to another as you had when you arrived.

The real demands of poverty are both subtler and more demanding. To give up the longing for things, to make a choice, even among necessary things, of what might be the plainest, the least appealing, is not easy. Then of course there was the nitty-gritty everyday practice of the virtue.

"Sister Eleanor, how many times do I have to tell you not to let the tap run... to turn off the lights when you leave the refectory... to lift your skirt going down stairs?" Sister Marie-Suzanne was a martinet when it came to taking care of things. I often stood shamefaced as she drew my deficiencies to my attention in front of the whole community. It might have been true enough that I was not acquisitive, but I was sloppy and careless both with my own things and, worse, with other people's.

Chastity was the vow and the virtue that defined most intimately the relationship with God, the possessor of our body, heart, and mind. We practised the vow and the virtue by loving God with all our being and being chaste and self-restrained. People often imagine, pruriently, that convents are hotbeds of suppressed sexuality, where lesbianism is the only outlet for all that pent-up desire. We were not so naïve as to imagine that physical relationships were unthinkable. I have no doubt that in my own congregation there were instances of extreme sentimental attachment and even sexual activity. What I did see plenty of, later, was the number of apparently mature women who developed ties of emotional dependency toward another nun, who became for them a surrogate mother or, subconsciously, a surrogate lover. This relationship not only clouded their judgment but gave rise to jealousy and resentment in their community. I thought this a far greater fault against chastity than the slightly flirtatious behaviour some nuns exhibited when in male company.

But one evening a remark by Sister Marie-Germaine at recreation threw me into a panic. Sister Odette was teasing me about entering a convent when I was so young. Surprisingly, Sister Marie-Germaine rushed to my defence, saying that youth was excellent. "Many of the greatest saints gave themselves to God before life tainted them," she stated. "Consecrated virginity is the greatest gift you can give to our Blessed Saviour."

My mouth dried and I lowered my head. I don't know if I blushed or paled, but I certainly knew my colour had changed. Thoughts chased frantically through my mind. Perhaps if I didn't say anything? How would anybody know? But then suppose my silence invalidated my vow?

I was so stunned I dropped my knitting. When, in my confusion, I eventually gathered it up, all the stitches had come off the needles and I had a tangled mess in my lap. It gave me an excuse not to look up, as with shaking fingers, my companions' conversation a confused drumming in my ears, I tried to gather both the stitches and my wits about me. At last, when I raised my head, I saw Sister Annie's big blue eyes fixed on me. She grinned slyly at me and I thought: *She's guessed.*

I tried to remember what Sister Mistress of Novices had actually said. *Had* she said virginity was a prerequisite for taking a vow of chastity? She had certainly spoken about consecrated virgins. I tried to put it all out of my mind, but I felt a little sick with apprehension as I waited for the monthly meeting with her. In her pleasant office, gripping my fingers tightly together, I blurted out, "I have to tell you, I'm not a virgin! I had a boyfriend. Does this mean I can't take a vow of chastity?" My mouth was dry and my pulse racing as I waited for her response.

She replied mildly, "Our Mother Foundress was a widow. You *know* the congregation admits widows. What's all this about, Sister?"

"Sister Marie-Germaine was speaking about consecrated virginity as if it was the same thing as taking a vow of chastity."

"You know it's not the same thing at all. There are hundreds of examples of saints who were not virgins, married people or reformed prostitutes, starting with Mary Magdalene. It is not necessary to be a virgin to take a vow of chastity. The past, whatever it was, is exactly that: the past. It is your present and future life that is important." She paused. "But there are perhaps things that you need to consider. Is continence likely to be an issue for you? It may well be more problematic. You have had a physical experience that you can't pretend never happened, something you enjoyed, an experience that you may long for again." She looked searchingly at me and I knew what she was asking.

"No. I don't miss it; I don't long for it, and if I did, I don't think I would feel any urge to do anything about it. But as you say, that experience is part of me. I can't just pretend it never happened."

"Then you could consider that your vow of chastity, when you make it, has another wonderful dimension. You have known the joy of physical passion and you must offer that too as a sacrifice, as an offering. How beautiful is that!"

"Well, I don't know that it was that great an episode; just blundering about in the dark really, both literally and figuratively. To tell the truth, I think I miss cigarettes more and I don't really miss them." I laughed with relief, and we passed on to other topics. I was a little short with Sister Annie a few days later, though, when she whispered tactlessly, "I didn't know we had our own Mary Magdalene among us!" She saw her mistake immediately and later had the grace to apologize, and the episode was closed.

Discussions about the meaning and the implications of the vows and community life were lively. It was just as well that there *were* topics to discuss, for recreation was not without its difficulties.

Attendance was obligatory and activities during this period of "relaxation" had to be communal, so reading or listening to music on your own or even with one or two others was not allowed. There was never any possibility of thinking: *I really could do without the company of my sisters today, so I think I'll push off for a bit of quiet time by myself*, and then going for a walk in the garden till one felt more sociable.

"My God, what would I give just to be by myself for a few hours every week!" Sister Susan burst out one day. She was pale and looked unwell. I knew she found community life a challenge. Things could be awkward. If there was something in particular you wanted to say to someone and it was going to take longer than a few minutes, it was surprisingly difficult to find a moment in private to do so. You almost had to book a time and actually prepare what you needed to say, and it had to be succinct: "Sister, I just want to say very quickly that I am sorry about…" or, "Sister, could you just tell me what you meant by… Perhaps you could tell me at evening recreation." Then the recipient had time to prepare *her* answer.

If our lectures were a great source of material for recreational conversation, so were the newspaper articles that sometimes formed part of the mealtime readings. The monumental events of the Second Vatican Council, which we had, exceptionally, followed on a television set up in Sacré-Coeur, kept us going for weeks, as did the assassination of President Kennedy the following year. Newspaper reporting of both these events eventually found its way into the novices' lavatories, where, torn into six-inch squares and threaded with string, the articles hung on a nail. Sometimes, infuriatingly, one had to search through a pile in order to find the end of an article. I imagine they were read with intense interest by all of us.

On fine days, afternoon recreation was spent outside, walking around the charmilles or helping Sister Eugenie with her little garden. One of the gardeners had made her a pretty little rustic bench from apple wood. It was delightful but insubstantial, and once, when a large sturdy novice sat down on it, the wretched thing collapsed under her like something out of a Buster Keaton film.

"Sister Eugenie, it was never strong," said Sister Annie, trying without success to halt the lamentations from the good old sister.

"It was for appearance only, not to be sat on," was the sharp reply.

When the bell rang for the rosary at the end of afternoon recreation, you fell into step with the sister nearest to you. In the spring and summer, the lovely avenues were nerve-racking for Sister Susan with her feather phobia, as the swallows flew like Spitfires just above our heads, catching the insects stirred up by our passage between the trees. She spent all her time ducking automatically at the sound of a wing.

Saying the rosary was one of the rare occasions that you found yourself alone with someone, though Sister Marie-Germaine always commented if she saw you praying three days running with the same novice. She seemed to feel that the prospect of "particular friendships" developing was an area where she should be especially vigilant. We thought she was obsessed about it.

"Friendship is good," she told us, "but particular friendships are a fault against the virtue of chastity and very detrimental to community life."

I thought it was nonsense. Surely "particular" is the very nature of friendship, and it seemed strange to me not to differentiate between an affectionate friendship and a dependent, emotional, or sexual one, the latter being what was being referred to with all this coded language about not seeking out the same companion too often for particular attention. Sister Mistress of Novices, on the other hand, was convinced that true and firm friendship was actually an antidote to what one might call unhealthy tendencies. It was perhaps unfortunate for her that it was in her temperament and nature to be both affectionate and partisan so that when I heard someone say once that she had favourites, and I knew myself to be one of them, I thought, possibly unfairly, that it undermined her stance on relationships.

CHAPTER 13

Music and a Pink Corset

We had choir practice twice a week in the music room, St Cecilia, to prepare for Sunday High Mass. Most novices were conscripted into the choir; actually you had to be pretty well atonal not to be. Gregorian plainchant is a very disciplined musical form. It doesn't allow for any individual interpretation or harmonization. It is not difficult to sing or even to read, but it is difficult to sing well.

Our model was the nearby Benedictine monastery of Solesmes. They had a particular style, a way of softening and lifting the end of each musical phrase, that made them easily identifiable. I once heard their singing described as "lugubrious" and although I don't agree with that, I can understand how some people were less than enchanted by their special muted delivery. Our lovely Choir Mistress, Sister Marie-Suzanne, thought they were wonderful, and her greatest aim was to have us sing as well, or nearly as well, as they did. She was very demanding and could be alarming if we didn't come up to scratch.

Once, during Mass, I hit two or even three wrong notes and, undone by her glare, laughed from sheer nervousness. At the post-Mass debriefing she tore our rendition to pieces, saying it was the worst sung Mass she had ever had the misfortune to conduct.

"And as for her," she hissed, pale with chagrin and gesticulating in my direction, "as for her, she had the gall to laugh!"

My heartfelt apologies were grudgingly accepted, but she made me sing the defective piece on my own. I did so with quavering uncertainty and she listened with grim satisfaction.

Eleanor on the morning of her "clothing", May 18 1962.

Eleanor and her mother on the day of Eleanor's "clothing".

The Mother House, in Evron, La Mayenne, France.

Sister Eleanor, summer 1966.

Sister Eleanor with her brother Peter, summer 1966.

The Sisters of Mary-Mount Community. *Left to right*: Sister Bernadette "Bernie", Sister Catherine, Sister Eleanor, Sister Mary (Sister Superior), Sister Philomena, Sister Maria, Sister Margaret-Mary, and Sister Isabelle, summer 1966.

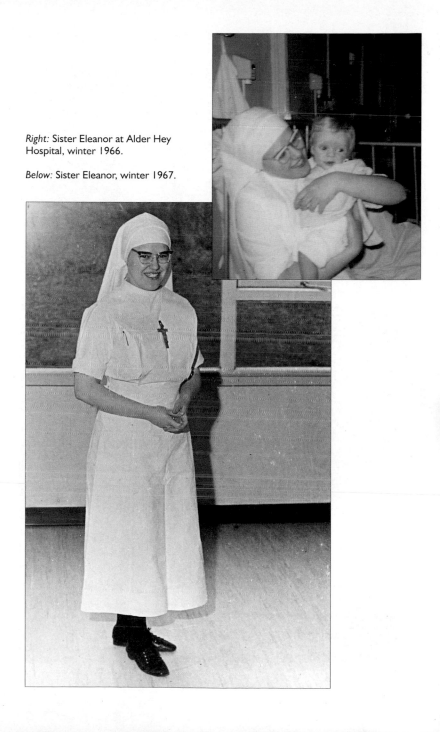

Right: Sister Eleanor at Alder Hey Hospital, winter 1966.

Below: Sister Eleanor, winter 1967.

Sister Eleanor (stood between Bessie Braddock, Labour MP for Liverpool, a nurse, and Matron) having received her State Registration.

She was always looking for ways to improve our technique and we were lucky enough to attend a two-day seminar of Gregorian music, at which Dom Gajard, the celebrated Choir Master at Solesmes, gave a master class. Nuns from all over the north of France attended. We were fascinated by the variety of habits, not just the style but the colour: the Dominicans, always elegant in black and white; some Franciscans in brown, others in grey; an American congregation, the Maryknoll Sisters, with frilled bonnets and shoulder capes; the Sisters of La Retraite, with coifs like little gothic chapels on their heads; the Cistercians, stunning all in white with voluminous cowls. There was also a very exotic group wearing sky blue. We envied them, although our own neat novices' habit with Peter Pan collar and creamy veil was admired. I think we got as much fun out of "spot the difference, name the congregation" as we did out of the seminars.

About once a month, theoretically, a visiting priest came to give us a talk. It was an eclectic series of lectures and we never knew the subject matter ahead of time. His talks were lively and intensely personal. Probably now I would find them self-indulgent. All his lectures seemed to emanate from some traumatic experience of his own. Guilt, he maintained, was a negative and possibly pathological condition.

"Psychiatric hospitals are full of people suffering from it," he declared. "Guilt has nothing to do with sorrow, regret, or real evil. Some of the most appalling human beings haven't felt any guilt at all, but an awareness of wrongdoing is a good thing to have; it is our moral compass, it allows us to differentiate right from wrong, and it puts us in touch with God." Leaning forward, his bony face intense, his thin hands gripping the edge of the little pulpit, his delivery was dramatic and compulsive; we were riveted, filled with something bordering on apprehension.

"He looks as if he is burning up with a sort of sacred fire," was Sister Odette's opinion one evening at recreation.

"He looks to me as if he could do with a darn good meal," said Sister Thérèse, "and a decent night's sleep." She was a restless, highly strung girl, prone to nightmares, shouting out in her sleep and grinding her teeth, so she was able, she said, to recognize insomnia when she saw it.

Periodically he would be absent for a few weeks and return pale and wan, his knobbly wrists projecting from his cuffs, his five-o'clock shadow very pronounced by the end of the afternoon. During one summer holiday, I read Georges Bernanos's *Diary of a Country Priest*. I thought it a sad and depressing book, but in the figure of the tormented anti-hero I knew our visiting priest.

There were other priests, equally dynamic, who came to talk to us. Once, an incredibly slovenly parish priest from Le Mans riveted us to our seats with his commentaries on aspects of the New Testament. I remember afterwards declaring with conviction, "That man has changed my life."

He had a terribly hammy delivery and a great sense of the dramatic, but every word rang with conviction. Sister Mistress of Novices told us that he had given sermons in the cathedral during the war, not stopping even during air raids. Striking an attitude and with raised finger he would thunder, "Listen to those angels of death and pray to your Redeemer." The sound of falling bombs and collapsing buildings added a sort of *deus ex machina* to the sermon.

If we had no lectures in the afternoon we were sometimes roped in to help in the garden to pick beans, which, in those pre-freezer days, were bottled in salt. The French bean grows close to the ground, unlike the tall and pretty red-flowered runner, so picking them was back-breaking work. We pinned up our blue aprons and filled the pouch with the deceptively light, slender vegetables. One hot afternoon, sweating and panting, I found myself groaning with backache and wondering how much longer I could go on. The others seemed tireless. We had been picking for about an hour and were still only half done.

"You're missing lots," hissed Sister Annie, passing me a handful. Looking over my shoulder, I saw the gleaners gathering up those I had missed and anticipated a reproach at the end of the afternoon, which couldn't come too soon. Ahead of me, Sister Eugenie, her sturdy legs astride the plants, picked steadily and apparently indefatigably.

Eventually she summoned me. "Whatever's the matter?" she asked crossly. "I've been listening to you groaning for about an hour. Are you ill?"

"It's my back," I said. "It feels as if it's breaking."

"You need some support. Come to see me in the sewing room after Vespers."

Vespers was an ordeal. My back complained every time it bent and straightened. At the doxology – "Glory be to the Father and to the Son and to the Holy Spirit" – we bowed from the waist a full ninety degrees. I was in some discomfort. Sister Odette to my left made sympathetic noises, but to my right Sister Annie and even Sister Susan sniggered.

"They cried out to the Lord in their distress," I chanted, "and he rescued them from it; he spoke the word and they were cured."

It was with a sigh of relief that I sank down in my seat for the fifteen minutes of meditation known as "the Visit" that followed Vespers.

In the sewing room, Sister Eugenie stripped me down to my chemise. With an expression in which contempt and astonishment were equally mixed, she pulled it up and whipped off my suspender belt.

"Ridiculous," she huffed, tossing it away. She produced her tape and measured me from below my bust to my hips. Still muttering to herself, she began to rummage in one of the long drawers in the cupboards that lined the wall and, having selected and then discarded several, eventually triumphantly produced an enormous pink corset. This was the real thing: not a roll-on or a girdle, but a real corset with whalebone, hooks and laces. She girded me with it. I stood meekly in my chemise and stockings, staring straight ahead, while she hooked it down the side and then, pressing with a strong hand in the small of my back, began to lace it up. It was all very nineteenth century. I half-expected Mammy from *Gone with the Wind* to breeze in.

I got instant relief from my backache and in fact it only took about a day or two to get used to the corset. It gave great support when there was heavy work to be done, rather like a weightlifter's belt, I suppose. An agreeable side effect was that it did encourage good posture. During Spiritual Reading I sat proud and tall. Sister Mistress of Novices smiled at me over the book and nodded, "Better?"

Conversation at recreation that night was almost bawdy. We learned that there was a corset on the market called "Scandal". Was I "scandalized", I was asked? Certainly the one I was wearing was a passion killer. I felt, however, that it might prove a great help, particularly for picking beans.

As we were going to bed, the house wrapped in the cocoon of the Great Silence, I thought unexpectedly of home, of sunny evenings in Oxford, of the bar in the Randolph and of the pub at the gates of Trinity where once, to my fury, the landlord had refused to serve me, undeceived by my faux sophistication. I wondered what on earth all those people I thought I knew so well, and who thought they knew me, would make of this strange way of life and of me living it, in particular the corset. Outside it was still light. I knelt to say my prayers, and through the open window above my head I heard the "plonk, plonk" of the toads in the garden. It sounded like water dripping into an empty bucket.

"Sweet Jesus," I prayed, "keep me here to love and serve you, even if I have to wear a hideous pink corset. Help me to do everything in your honour, even if it's picking beans. Let me see you in everyone I meet tomorrow, even Sister Marie-Germaine – above all Sister Marie-Germaine." My back gave a twinge as I got into bed. "Give me a good night's sleep despite a surfeit of macaroni cheese." I fell asleep, my mind calm and easy, but the heavy supper played havoc with my digestion till the early hours.

Chapter 14

Holiday Time

The summer months always seemed busier than the rest of the year. From about June onwards, large groups of sisters began to arrive at three weekly intervals to make their annual retreat. As novices, we were conscripted into helping in the general preparation, which we all found great fun. Among the participants at these six-day events it became easy to identify those who were natural "prefect" material. It was interesting to see how the same nuns turned up as group leaders or "spokes-nuns" when there were conferences, another community event.

"Have you noticed," remarked Sister Odette, "how there is always someone ready to tell the others what to do?"

"Yes, and it's usually Sister Marie-Germaine. She's in her element and very efficient and popular." Sister Susan's observations about our Postulant Mistress were usually uttered with amused affection.

Our own daily timetable had to be slotted into that of the visitors.

"You realize," Sister Annie pointed out gleefully, "this means we get an extra half hour in bed? The sisters on retreat don't get up till 6:00 a.m. and as our rising bell would disturb them, we get an extra lie-in as well." The only other occasion, apart from illness, when we gained that precious half hour was when we were menstruating, and then we were entitled to a brief lie-in on the strength of what was called, with a charming euphemism, our "bad days".

Sister Marie-Suzanne hated the disruption. Her calm orderly temperament thrived on regularity. The unavoidable changes to the routine threw her out and she became cross and was sharp with us, so that we in our turn became jumpy. When a bell rang and we began automatically to close our books, she would snap crossly, "It isn't for you, it isn't for you!" She got so used to doing this that, on more than one occasion, she was wrong and we arrived late for meals, much to her consternation.

When the retreats were over, the noviciate in its entirety left the Mother House and went on holiday. It was a major operation. We took not only our personal belongings, but kitchen equipment and several tea chests, one filled with non-perishable food and another with our hymn books, sheet music, several recorders, and Sister Eugenie's sewing machine. The two coaches made a detour to pick up mattresses.

Our destination was a pretty little hamlet deep in the countryside. The accommodation was part of a delightful *maison de maître* (gentleman's residence) on loan to the congregation. The whole place looked enchanting: a sandy courtyard enclosed by an L-shaped house and a little copse. The only access to the first floor of the low range of buildings, which we were allocated, was by a narrow twisting staircase at one end, so it was immediately obvious that getting the mattresses up to the bedrooms was going to be tricky. The mattresses themselves, although thin and narrow, were stiff, and resisted all attempts to bend them. In the end we tied a rope around each one and hauled them laboriously up through the windows.

Upstairs we found a large room full of iron bedsteads with wire spring bases, giving a barrack room appearance, though we greeted it with exclamations of pleasure. There was a rustic appeal in the low ceiling, the whitewashed walls and simple furnishings. We soon realized that the accommodation was even more basic than we had first thought. As there was no plumbing above stairs, water was supplied for washing in large enamel jugs that we took it in turns to collect from the kitchen on the ground floor. In the corridor, a long trestle table furnished with bowls served as a washroom. The lavatories also were downstairs and as nocturnal wanderings were discouraged, and indeed would have been frankly dangerous due to the precipitate nature of the stairs and the dim lighting in the narrow passages, we were reduced to the china potty if we woke in the night. This involved the humiliating trip to "slop out" in the morning. The French, I think, have a much more robust attitude to natural functions than the Anglo-Saxons and seemed quite unembarrassed by the daily procession of those who couldn't go through the night. I always found it humiliating!

"I don't have a weak bladder," I explained to Sister Annie, who as usual was giggling. "I've got strong kidneys!"

In bed that first night I found the mattress had a sweet, not unpleasant, slightly musty smell, confirming my belief that they were stuffed with straw. I thought that those of an asthmatic tendency might suffer, what with the straw combined with the dust emanating from the ticking. Certainly I heard a lot of sneezing.

Typically the first thing we had to do was clean everything once we had settled in. Previous holiday guests had left the usual detritus. Opening a cupboard on a low sideboard the first morning Sister Paule let out a cry of horror as a large grass snake dropped to the floor and, hissing furiously, disappeared out into the courtyard and vanished into the vegetation at the edge. It left an acrid smell behind it.

Sister Agnès reassured us, "They like water. There must be a stream nearby. They are quite harmless." We were not particularly reassured. Sister Paule was pale with shock, and we all spent some time peering around very carefully. The prospect of finding another one was too horrid to contemplate. The grass snake was clearly as frightened by us as we were of it, though, and we never saw another one.

The fortnight we spent in that delightful bucolic place was pure innocent pleasure. We rose at 7:00 a.m., a real change from the usual half-past five, although it took several days to get used to it. There were no curtains at the windows, so I woke early every morning to bright daylight and relished the pleasure of lying comfortably in bed, listening either to the gentle breathing of those more able to take advantage of the delayed bell or to the evident restlessness of those who, like me, were already awake. After several days, we all adapted and slept till the 7:00 a.m. alarm jangled us awake.

The Office and our routine of prayers were adapted in a tranquil manner to fit in with the holiday. Every morning we walked down the little lane behind the house to Mass in the village church. Each day the parish priest came out from the church to welcome us, the first day with tears in his eyes. His daily Mass was sometimes attended by one or two devout parishioners; usually he was on his own. If the bourgeoisie has remained resolutely Catholic, the same cannot be said for the rest of French society. Even in the countryside there had been a steady fall in church attendance. We were certainly objects of curiosity. More than twenty white-veiled novices, most of them young and some extremely pretty, with several older but fit and confident women, drew an audience comprising, among others, the curious, the speculative, and even the ribald, though the latter only hovered on the fringes.

I tried smiling, I hope winningly, at them all, until pulled up smartly by Sister Marie-Germaine. "What are doing, Sister Eleanor?" she demanded one morning. "Why are you looking at people and smiling like that? What have I told you about keeping a guard on your eyes?"

"I am just trying to show them that under our habits we are just ordinary people, Sister."

She drew her breath in sharply. "We are *not* ordinary people; we are nuns, or in your case a novice! Modesty and humility – that's what you should be aiming for!"

"Oh heavens," I thought, "will I ever get this right!"

On the way back from Mass we passed a flourishing vegetable garden with a large open cistern. Hollyhocks and valerian grew in great blowsy drifts along the wall that enclosed it, and water lilies covered the surface. Several of us commented about it during the day, with the kind of casual easy comments that one makes about pleasant surroundings. The next couple of days were particularly humid and we all agreed how pleasant it was to have the shade of the trees and water close by. However, at night the mosquitoes rose in their thousands from that beautiful lily-covered cistern. Having easily identified us as a source of fresh warm blood, unprotected even by curtains, they homed in on us. We rose the next morning either blotched with bites or covered with a heat rash, from having spent the night with our heads buried beneath the covers. Help came from an unexpected source. On about night four, once the lights were out, two little bats flew into the dormitory and although several novices found them almost as unacceptable as the mosquitoes (Sister Thérèse shrieked and buried her head under her pillow) they considerably reduced our nightly visitation and made our sleep easier.

Holidays in a convent world have a structure and a purpose almost as disciplined as a working week. They are considered to be for rest and recuperation, possibly relaxation. They are not for the idle passage of time, nor to be filled with trivia. In fact trivia is an unknown concept in the religious life. So although we were on holiday and relaxed, and indeed enjoyed independent free time with periods when we could find a quiet place to read or just be alone, in general the days were highly organized.

Apart from the cooking done by those chosen for their culinary competence, there was still housework. Not for us the unmade bed nor the untidy cupboard. Standards were maintained. But there was fun too. Long walks and picnics were daily events. Two or three would go ahead on bicycles to the pre-determined rendezvous with bread strapped to the carriers, pots of rillettes, cheese, wine, and cider in the baskets, and the rest of us followed on foot. Once, we found a small warm lake with a smooth, shallow, sandy edge and several of us pulled off shoes and stockings and paddled like children, until Sister Marie-Germaine called us to order. All deviation from the norm had to be authorized. We came out with tiny black leeches clinging to our feet, which proved surprisingly resistant to being removed.

Sometimes during a walk we found wild strawberries and then one day hundreds of mushrooms, which the country novices among us fell upon with exclamations of delight.

"We're not going to eat them?" I demanded in horror. I didn't recognize any and was convinced they were poisonous. Sister Paule looked at me with pity and then patiently began to identify them for me. She was still periodically expressing not just astonishment but dismay about the culinary defects of English cuisine – information she had gleaned from me.

Sometimes, sleepy with sun, cider, and a long walk, we would spread out to find quiet spots to dream or snooze. From these walks, we would return to Vespers, Spiritual Reading, and suppers of vegetable soup, artichokes with vinaigrette and béchamel sauce, or hot chestnuts in milk, salad and cheese and often the suspicious mushrooms. Recreation was friendly and easy, which was not always the case in Evron, where occasionally tedious events of the day could surface in petty irritation and acrimony. Once, carried away as usual by a lack of judgment and a reluctance to end a perfect day, Sister Odette and I decided to take a turn in the copse after Compline, before turning in. The holiday spirit had got to me, so we were both taken aback when we were accosted by a very irate Sister Mistress of Novices, who demanded to know what we thought we were doing ambling in the dark (it was actually still broad daylight) and ignoring the Great Silence. She was not always gently ironic! Chastened, we went to bed. The Rule was always the Rule.

Once during that halcyon holiday we were invited to attend a special Mass being celebrated in a chapel in the country. We walked for about an hour through fields heavy with wheat and came to a very old and dilapidated little chapel. We were surprised to find a great gathering of people and stunned to discover that the majority were young. Not only young, but dressed as if for a party! Girls in high heels with bouffant hairdos darted around, their full, coloured skirts bouncing and swirling as they formed little giggling groups, then broke up to form other giggling groups. Around the fringes stood young men in twos or threes, their suits too tight and their heavy shoes still dust covered. They looked sheepish and embarrassed, watching the girls covertly and smoking, their cigarettes cupped in their palms. Although the girls ignored them it was clear that all the rustling activity was for them. There were a few older country people, farmers and their wives, and some local tradesmen. Beyond the chapel there was an open marquee, with long tables down each side and what was obviously a dance floor in the middle. The marquee and the trees around were festooned with bunting, and bales of hay were spread out under them. It looked idyllic.

"Doesn't that look lovely," I said admiringly. "It's like a painting! It should be called *Country Dance*."

"It's for a ball this evening." Sister Annie's voice was heavy with disapproval. I had heard this opprobrium before when balls were mentioned and been puzzled. Balls in my experience were glamorous and elegant affairs. This event was clearly not of that order. Was a ball the same thing as a dance, which I associated with the village youth club, the Young Farmers or, even more jolly, the Young Conservatives? It didn't sound the same thing at all, yet why should a dance be so disapproved of?

"They aren't good places to go," she whispered. "The music is a stimulant and young people forget that…" Her voice trailed off. Clearly French balls were very different from our innocent and daringly flirtatious affairs. It sounded positively Bacchanalian. My sister novices spoke of these events as if they were unbridled orgies.

Not for the first time, I wondered if this was a French thing, but, as I soon learned, it was a religious thing. Overall for Catholics, the received wisdom was "spirit good; flesh bad". The church was only just beginning to move away from the general conviction that we were always at risk of being betrayed by our bodies, and by our bodies the church meant, above all, sex. In the list of the seven deadly sins, lust comes first and, for any Catholic, it is probably the only one that they can remember. For the devout, "balls" were "occasions of sin". In other words, "the opportunity for sin"; the risk of sinning was so great that it was better to avoid the situation entirely. Occasion of sin or not, this event had brought more youngsters to Mass than anything in the village, and I said so.

"Yes," replied Sister Annie firmly, "but they have only come for the ball."

"Well," interjected Sister Odette, never one to let Sister Annie's comments pass, "you don't know any more than me *what* they've come for; so we must hope the Father gives a brilliant sermon and that they hear something to their advantage."

Poor Annie blushed and looked hurt. She found Sister Odette's sharp ripostes difficult to cope with and her blue eyes filled with tears. I felt sorry for her. She was vulnerable and more deserving of support than of Sister Odette's scathing remarks.

"You ought to be kinder to her," I whispered. "You've hurt her. Where's your charity? She's very sweet, never unkind or spiteful."

"Unlike me, I suppose you mean!"

"Well..." I looked at her with my eyebrows raised. She pursed her lips, but had the grace to look a little ashamed.

Inside the chapel, flaking whitewashed walls and the peculiar damp smell associated with places little used and rarely aired gave it a sad and decaying atmosphere. The congregation crowded in: the young men uneasy at the back and the girls self-importantly at the front. They stared at us novices with a not unfriendly amusement bordering on contempt, and made what I took to be sniggering comments about us behind their hands.

Mass progressed at a normal pace. Then came the event that was to leave Sister Susan and me dumbfounded. As the priest unveiled the chalice and began the prelude to the sacrament proper, four of the girls rose, genuflected winningly and disappeared toward the back of the chapel. I thought they had gone to take the collection. Not at all; after a while they reappeared at the end of the pews with baskets filled with quite substantial pieces of brioche. Looking behind me, I saw that everybody in the chapel was eating brioche. I was stunned. This was 1962; the rules covering fasting before taking communion were still very strict. There was no eating or drinking from midnight until after Mass, although anyone on medication was exempt. For the young and healthy, eating brioche ten minutes before communion meant we would break our fast. I refused the basket, as did Sister Susan. Sister Marie-Germaine, vigilant as ever, hissed along the pew and indicated that we were to take a piece. As I wasn't sure what was to happen next – maybe none of us were going to communion – I ate my brioche with some hesitation. When the moment of communion came, everyone went to the altar.

As nobody else seemed in the least perturbed, I began to calm down and everybody including me took communion. Afterwards I spoke to Sister Mistress of Novices.

"Yes," she said, "it did seem odd, but this is obviously something to do with a very old country tradition and as the priest was there and didn't put up an objection, we must assume it is all right."

So we left the *fête champêtre* and the revellers to their ball and I hoped then, as I do now, that they had a lovely time and that the "occasion of sin" didn't prove too compelling.

The incident with the brioche at Mass made me aware how differently the Catholic traditions were observed in France and in England. Converts to the faith, in particular, took their Catholicism very seriously indeed and had none of the easy tolerance and lazy scepticism that those born in the faith, particularly in France, seemed to develop. For example, priests in England were held in high regard. Nobody laughed at priests, much less criticized them, but in France a buffoon was a buffoon, and a pompous priest could easily become an object of ridicule, even if his priesthood was respected.

An earlier event that occurred when I was a postulant seemed to illustrate the national difference in what you might call spirituality. The basilica in the town was dedicated to Our Lady. Legend had it that a relic purported to be a vial containing Our Lady's breast milk had been brought there by a pilgrim from Jerusalem. Once a year the novices went to the basilica to venerate this dubious object.

I thought the whole thing farcical, but Sister Susan was outraged. Raised as a Protestant, she was probably ambivalent about relics in general, but one that was so obviously phoney was completely unacceptable and she refused to go. Sister Marie-Germaine's irritation with what she considered obstinacy, or possibly a fault against the virtue of obedience, only exacerbated the stand-off. Sister Odette, in the face of Sister Susan's distress, agreed that the whole thing was ridiculous, but even if it wasn't the Virgin's milk, was it not possible that it was some relic from the Holy Land? And anyway a visit to the basilica was always a pleasure. Sister Susan was not so easily reassured. In the end, we all went and duly recited the prayers of the little service. When the time came for the kissing and honouring of the relic, Sister Susan remained stony-faced in her seat and we all sheepishly, and in retrospect I think cravenly, venerated a small glass vial containing something that resembled dried mud.

These two events – the country Mass with the brioche that nobody had any hesitation about and the veneration of a dubious relic – both of them "traditional", encapsulated for me the pragmatic nature of French Catholicism. It believed there were hoops to be jumped through but that God could cope with all this nonsense, and that there were far more important things to be going on with. It was another "black pudding" moment.

CHAPTER 15

Crisis

After the holiday there were more disruptions to our routine. A succession of conferences normally lasting two or three days brought the customary influx of nuns from all the provinces.

It wasn't always a priest who headed the conferences; we had an industrialist once and painfully dull he was too. I remember a talk of mind-numbing tedium on *le grève et le lock-out* (strikes and lock-outs). He was, thankfully, an exception. Most speakers were excellent.

The discussions that followed the lectures were often very animated. We were, we believed, witnessing the start of a new impetus, a great renewal in the church. We certainly felt that the Holy Ghost was breathing down our necks. There was increasingly a feeling, though still vague, that nuns and the laity should be working together in a new dynamic way.

Nuns, contrary to general understanding of their place in the church, are not "clerical" at all. They are not part of the priesthood; they are secular, although secular in a very particular way. It is the vows and their community life that sets them apart from the general body of the laity. This led occasionally to bizarre behaviour. In some congregations, nuns neither ate nor drank as much as a sweet or a cup of tea in public. It was as if they wished to give the impression that they were above such physical activity.

By the time I entered my convent in 1961 the custom of wearing an all-enveloping garment in the bath, lest one catch a glimpse of one's own flesh and be tempted to lustful thoughts, had been abandoned. But the idea that anyone should come upon you even in the most modest state of undress was still unthinkable. Once, at Filey, I came across the cook having just returned from Mass, unpinning her veil. She took it off and began to fold it while standing talking to me. For Mass the sisters wore a long fine veil over the ordinary shorter one. She thought she was taking the long one off, which would leave her head covered with the ordinary short one. Instead (presumably she had forgotten that she had already removed the long veil) she took off her ordinary veil and was therefore veil-less and had only her white bonnet on. She was perfectly covered up. Her white bandeau, which covered her head and brow, was immaculately clean. She looked neat and respectable, not unlike the painting of Whistler's mother. When she realized what she had done, she let out such a shriek that I felt immediately that, even by witnessing this, I had been party to some appalling lapse in religious behaviour. She ran from me in horror, her hands over her head, and though she returned to the kitchen almost immediately, the offending article securely in place, she never referred to the incident again. The removal of her veil was clearly a hideous faux pas. In her eyes it was tantamount to taking off her dress and standing in her underwear.

Sister Odette told me that a nun who had to be hospitalized for any reason often wore a sort of modified habit in bed, complete with bonnet and veil. "What's more," she said, "they are even accompanied into the operating theatre by another sister, who only leaves once they are unconscious." I wasn't sure if she was teasing me, so replied, dismissively, that our sisters prided themselves on being more down to earth. I certainly hoped they were. In France nuns ate quite happily in public and even the North American sisters were much more relaxed about that than their English counterparts. I remembered that in the Yorkshire convent I had eaten alone.

Despite our vocation to our specific congregation, many felt that we should be aiming for the kind of life being led by some of the newer religious communities, who worked in factories, in agriculture, or other blue collar organizations, and whose vocation was simply to provide, to demonstrate, a Christian presence. Their aim was not to proselytize, but to work alongside the lower paid, even the lowest paid, in a spirit of comradeship and participation. Like the worker-priest, they shared the social environment of the area they lived in. The experiment of the worker-priests had been ultimately unsuccessful. Rome refused to ratify it. Many felt sad and not a few very bitter, but the idea and the ideal were never completely abandoned and would resurface a decade or so later in liberation theology. Again it was contentious, but the church has not been untouched by it and this theological movement has many adherents and some martyrs.

In our animated discussions and youthful enthusiasm, we tossed these ideas around at these conferences until we convinced ourselves that we were on the verge of such a brave new world that nothing could halt or delay its inception.

These views were the underlying cause of the considerable disharmony that arose in some areas of the congregation. Indeed, as we later discovered, the congregation in France was divided into roughly two camps: one deeply loyal and attached to Reverend Mother General, a traditional and conservative figure, and a second group, mainly but not exclusively, of young nuns who had come under the influence of the current Sister Mistress of Novices. She had been Sister Superior at our big school in Le Mans. This establishment had always had a reputation for being non-traditional, even avant-garde, probably because of its highly academic and artistic community. At least two nuns held doctorates and the art teacher was nationally recognized. The convent was viewed with suspicion by some in the congregation.

There was particular resentment that the most recent additions to the congregation, "the novices", should feel any dissatisfaction with the status quo. If they didn't like the way things were done here, why had they joined? Sister Mistress of Novices was seen by many as at fault, first for not calling us to order and secondly (and worse) for encouraging both our "radical" views and our outspokenness at the conferences. So, although not overt, there was considerable disagreement between those who longed for root and branch renewal, and those who valued the traditions of a very old and respected organization. The latter believed that the congregation had already made considerable adaptations to the modern world and all that was needed at the most was a little further adjustment. Political infighting, as I was later to learn, was alive and well and thriving in the Mother House.

In the autumn, four new postulants arrived, one an English girl. Eighteen-year-old Clare was rosy-cheeked and fun-loving; she was a great addition to our community. Jeannine and Georgette were both young too. The fourth was a woman in her forties, whose frail health seemed from the start to suggest she was unlikely to stay the course.

Sister Marie-Germaine was immediately a happier woman. She had her postulants and a purpose; being needed brought out the best in her. So we were back to her bustling energetic presence. She was extraordinarily kind to the older sickly postulant, tolerant and encouraging. Sadly, the old pattern of harshness and ill-concealed dislike repeated itself in her relationship with Sister Jeannine, who was prepared to go head to head with her. Sister Clare's sunny nature and pragmatism allowed her to ride many a storm, and Sister Georgette seemed to manage to stay to some extent below the parapet. Certainly Sister Marie-Germaine's involvement with the newcomers spared us her frequent critical incursions into Sacré-Coeur.

Unexpectedly I faced a crisis of my own. I began to suffer from devastating insomnia. I would fall asleep, only to wake an hour later and find it impossible to drop off again. If I did, my sleep was so shallow I woke every quarter of an hour to hear the basilica clock remind me how little time I had before the rising bell at 5:30 a.m. This pattern repeated itself for three or so days until, exhausted, I would sleep the sleep of the dead and wake reasonably refreshed, only for the whole cycle to begin again.

Combined with this, I was overcome with a dull lack of feeling. All the sparkle and enthusiasm of the last few months, my joy at being a novice, my conviction that I had well and truly found my place, my certainty of my vocation, didn't so much ebb away as cease to have any meaning. The saints tell us that, in such circumstances, it is essential to carry on as usual, doing what has to be done in prayer and in work. In the end, they say, all will resolve itself.

In theory this is all very well, but in practice it is not so easy. I didn't want to pray; I didn't want to work; all I wanted to do was sleep. As if this wasn't enough, I caught flu and was bedridden for a week. I felt so unwell the first few days that I was happy just to lie in misery but, after a week, I was bored beyond belief. In convents, bed is a place for rest, so I was deprived of the luxury of any reading material, apart from my Office Book and my Bible.

In the end, anything was preferable to lying in bed, so unsteadily and certainly prematurely, I went downstairs. It was the beginning of a very hard time. Even when I was up again and apparently better, I dragged myself around, listless and depressed. Even the thought of Advent and the preparations for Christmas, which I had so enjoyed the previous year, didn't lift my spirits. My interior life was a desert; I remembered Gerard Manley Hopkins' line "Mine, O thou lord of life, send my roots rain". I felt parched, arid. God, who had become a living loving presence, seemed horribly absent.

Sister Mistress of Novices was very kind and encouraging and dosed me with chloral drops on sugar lumps before bedtime, in what proved to be a vain attempt to alleviate my wretched nights, but in the end even she began to find it difficult to sustain cheerfulness in the face of my sullen moroseness, particularly as the medication did nothing to alleviate the crushing insomnia.

There were days when I felt more myself, when my mood lifted, but it took very little to reduce me to sour self-pity. This attitude was viewed with some speculation, certainly by Sister Marie-Suzanne. Her cool detached regard plunged me into further trepidation, and my fear that I might be on my way home to England deepened. This appalling thought hung over me like the spectre of Yvonne, who had left us so abruptly when we were postulants, and yet I was incapable of pulling myself out of my despondency.

Help came through the most unlikely set of circumstances. Occasionally, some visiting dignity would be asked to give a talk to the whole community. One gloomy December evening, we were called to the Chapter Room of the Mother House to listen to a missionary priest tell of his life in the Ivory Coast and Chad. The talk was dreadful. Apart from the fact that it was dull, it was imbued with outdated old colonial attitudes. Today it would be considered racist. The speaker was clearly very fond of his "children", but spoke of them with a deeply unpleasant patronizing paternalism. The whole hour that we listened to him did nothing to stimulate our admiration for the work to which he had dedicated himself for so many years.

As his talk progressed, I began to feel increasingly irritated and restless. I began to mutter below my breath, to shift around in my place, to sigh noisily and to snigger behind my hand. Worse, I involved poor Sister Paule, who was sitting next to me, in my activities. She was clearly embarrassed by my nudging and whispering, and attempted to subdue me, but I was beyond it. This whole episode was an exercise on my part in self-indulgence, vanity, and bad manners.

The talk was followed by Benediction in the chapel, at which the little priest was to be the celebrant. In his honour, he was dressed in all the richest and most decorated vestments. The vast stiff cope trailed behind him as he approached the altar. The moment for the blessing with the vessel containing the Eucharist arrived; the Sister Sacristan placed the equally stiff embroidered stole around his shoulders, the sacristy bell rang, and we bowed our heads and waited for the bell to ring again to announce the blessing was over. We waited and waited and waited. Suddenly I felt a sharp dig in my ribs from Sister Annie on my left and looked up. The poor little priest was hobbled by the stiff stole which had slipped from his narrow shoulders and pinned him around the knees. He was helpless: he couldn't put the vessel down as he was in front of the altar, and he risked tumbling down the altar steps. He was as hog-tied as if he were a parcel. Sister Sacristan was on her knees in front of him, unhooking whatever needed to be unhooked in order to free him. I was filled with a malicious glee at his predicament, and I laughed aloud.

A couple of days later I was summoned. Sister Mistress of Novices stood at the window in her office, a cup of tea in her hand. She didn't look at me. She had, she informed me, received a summons herself. As my Novice Mistress, she had been asked by Reverend Mother General to explain my "extraordinary behaviour" both during a lecture given by a most respectable priest who was a guest in the Mother House (*guest* was heavily emphasized) and afterwards during Benediction when I had thought it appropriate to laugh at his discomfiture. I stood silent, not daring to meet her eyes.

"I explained to Reverend Mother," she said icily, "that although Sister Eleanor understands perfectly the theory and the spirit of the religious life, she appears at the moment to be quite incapable of practising it."

I was dumb with horror. It was not that the episode in itself was so monstrous; it was my blinding realization of my crass stupidity. "Oh God," I wept, bursting into tears, "I'm a fool, such a fool." I wanted to put my head down on something, to abase myself; to show my shame, my regret, my contrition. The only thing handy was a small table next to where I was standing, so I put my head down on that. I must have looked both uncomfortable and ridiculous, and for all I know Sister Mistress of Novices was smiling. Her voice, however, was not.

"Absolutely," she said. "An absolute fool." She continued, "You have been unwell, sleeping badly, finding it difficult to throw off the effects of flu, but *this* is not a health issue. You can't excuse your behaviour on those grounds. No, this is you; this is Eleanor with her lack of judgment, her impertinence, her thoughtlessness, her lack of modesty, her desire to be noticed.

"Your behaviour was unacceptable on several counts," she continued. "You were rude to a guest, and to a very old and frail one at that, a man furthermore who has spent most of his life for the love of Jesus Christ in the service of the church. So you didn't like his attitude. Do you imagine you alone were the only person who deplored his view of the African people? Suppose we had all sniggered. Do you know so much about the problems of the mission field that you thought fit to judge him? Finally, you took pleasure in his discomfiture, a poor old priest, happy to wear our most beautiful vestments and delighted to be asked to give Benediction, and who suddenly found himself ridiculous. Do you think he was not embarrassed? Common courtesy demands that we pretend not to notice."

By this time I was not crying. I was beyond tears. I was overwhelmed with embarrassment and a deep shame. This was me being revealed in all my shallowness; this I knew was the truth.

She dismissed me ruthlessly, and her parting shot was no comfort: "Don't come to me for advice or comfort and certainly not for reassurance. This is something you must resolve by yourself; and with God's help, of course." This last sounded to me a bit of an afterthought, as if she believed, I thought in my wretchedness, that even God was going to find it a challenge.

For nearly two weeks I wandered around in a mist of bemusement, just going through the motions. The routine was my mainstay; at least I didn't have to think what to do next. Then I truly began to pray. Not with words but with an inward yearning for God to transform me into what he wanted me to be. So deep was the desire to address my faults that for some time I was almost in danger of scrupulousness, that obsessional picking over of faults both real and imaginary, which (like guilt) can be pathological. I was saved, I believe, by that most neglected member of the Godhead, the Holy Ghost, that dazzling bright Spirit who brings us comfort, wisdom and love. Prayers to the "Paraclete", the Comforter, are among the most beautiful in the Liturgy and the memory of them brought me immeasurable reassurance at that dark time. Like St Thomas More, I wanted to "lean into the comfort of God… to labour to love Him".

Ebullient, chirpy Eleanor was, at least for some time, remote, separate, and unbelievably quiet, which was probably some relief to the community. My fellow novices, who could not have failed to notice that something was clearly off key, supported me with cheerful, unfailing kindness and unspoken sympathy. Gradually some equilibrium and peace of mind returned.

Leaving the refectory after breakfast one morning, I bumped into Sister Mistress of Novices. We looked at each other.

"I'm better," I said.

"So I see," she replied. "Perhaps we can talk about it when you next come to see me."

My only clear reference to what had happened was to ask, "Should I write a letter of apology to Reverend Mother General?"

"Oh, I shouldn't think so. She has almost certainly forgotten about it and you would be ill advised," she added, with her typically ironic tone of voice, "to recall to her mind your truly appalling behaviour. Anonymity – that's what you should be aiming for." And so the episode was closed.

At last I began to sleep better, the after effects of the flu diminished, and suddenly it was Christmas again.

CHAPTER 16

Death and Sister Pauline

In a convent there is no event more solemn and no ritual more beautifully staged than death. Death is the door to eternity and the entrance, one hopes, to paradise. This will be the ultimate intimate encounter when man or woman meets the main Mover and Shaker of the here below and the hereafter. And so in religious houses, death is not to be feared or dreaded and, if not exactly welcomed (it is a brave soul who doesn't feel some trepidation about a lonely journey into the unknown), the inevitable is usually accepted with a peaceful resignation. At least that is the theory.

The infirmary was a gentle retirement home for elderly or incapacitated sisters; consequently there were a great many deaths. Some were sudden, but for the most part there was a slow slipping away, so the community had time to prepare for them.

A very slow tolling bell was the signal that a sister in the infirmary was receiving the Last Rites. All inessential work stopped for the space of a few minutes and we recited the *De profundis* and the *Miserere mei, Deus*, the penitential Psalms 130 and 51. If the dying nun heard the bell, she would know that the entire community was united with her in love and prayer. I came across one or two unpleasant nuns in my day, but no matter what the personality, the temperament, or behaviour of any given individual, at that hour, those prayers were our duty and her right.

One sunny afternoon, returning from the laundry on the weekly trip to collect the bed linen, winding our way back through the garden, we heard the bell tolling on the terrace. Careful not to drop the sheets, we knelt on the dusty path while Sister Eugenie and Sister Marie-Suzanne intoned the prayers. Across the garden I saw Sister Bernadette put down her hoe and kneel as well. Above us on the terrace one of the workmen, leading the donkey and cart, rested his hand on the rump of the animal and, pulling off his cap, stood with bowed head. It was poignant and dignified. Unfortunately at that moment someone dropped all her sheets and the penultimate line of the *De profundis* was interrupted by Sister Marie-Suzanne's admonition, so it came out as: "For with the Lord there is mercy, and with him is plenteous redemption... Sister, take them all back to the laundry. They must all go through again. You *will* be popular... and he will redeem Israel from all their iniquities." Yet again we began to giggle.

"She takes it very hard," Sister Marie-Germaine told us. "She weeps all the time; she feels it so." She was speaking of Reverend Mother General, who together with the Council always attended the dead bed anointing. I didn't think this would help the sister-in-extremis very much. Although Sister Marie-Germaine obviously wanted us to see this as a sign of Reverend Mother General's tenderness of heart, I felt it showed a disappointing lack of control and, in later years when my judgment may have been harsher, some degree of self-indulgence. Certainly at the funerals that followed she always appeared composed and her eyes were dry, if red.

The funerals were dramatic. Simple and down to earth as our congregation was, we certainly knew how to rise to the occasion. When the doors of the cloister swung open for the first funeral Mass I attended, my breath caught in my throat. On either side of the cloister the community were lined up: silent, cloaked, motionless, black and white against the grey walls; it was intensely, almost theatrically, dramatic.

The coffin stood in the centre on stark trestles, draped in a purple pall with a large silver crucifix atop. At the head of the coffin stood Reverend Mother General flanked by the councillors. We took our places too against the walls. The silence was not oppressive. It was peaceful but it was absolute. Reverend Mother and the Council turned to enter the chapel and four pall-bearers, the gardeners, who had been waiting in the cloister garden, slipped in to take the coffin, which was met at the door by the chaplain, who blessed it before leading it in. We fell into line behind and followed.

We knew the Requiem Mass well, as it was the one we sang most often. The melody was similar to the Easter Mass so, although solemn, was joyful. It was above all dramatic. The Second Vatican Council eventually got rid of the wonderful sequence hymn *Dies irae, dies illa* (Day of wrath, day of mourning), with its plea for mercy, its acknowledgment of sin, its longing for paradise, and its fear of damnation. It was powerful and emotive, like so much of the old rubric that has been abandoned, some might say lost.

The drama of the whole event was so intense it was a relief to get out into the fresh air, so we accompanied the coffin along the terrace and through the charmilles to the little cemetery. Again the choreography was well established: we lined the ivy-draped walls and chanted for the last time the *De profundis*, with the sweet doxology "Eternal rest give unto her, O Lord, and let perpetual light shine upon her. May she rest in peace", and the chaplain recited the prayers for the committal. We left the grave to the workmen; the pall had been folded and the plain deal coffin looked stark against the piled earth.

The funeral that stuck in my mind was that of Sister Pauline, she of the shop-lifting at the Christmas bazaars. All through our noviciate she had been a source of amusement and distraction. Her senility had a childlike charm about it, at least for those of us who didn't have to live with it on a day-to-day basis. We found her irresistible. She was like a sparrow, with her sharp little nose and beady brown eyes, and for some unknown reason was drawn to us. Maybe in her confusion she thought she was still a novice. We often found her hovering around the front door or waiting earnestly for us near the Mother House kitchen when she knew we were coming for the meal trays. She would pop up occasionally in the garden, appearing from behind a tree or from inside one of the numerous little chapels scattered around the grounds. Shuffling toward us, beaming widely, babbling away, completely incoherent, she was immune to the scolding she inevitably incurred.

"You are not supposed to talk to the novices. Off you go," Sister Eugenie would say crossly. But Sister Pauline, for all her dementia, was what the French call *espiègle* (mischievous) and usually knew when she could catch us alone. Her pockets were always full of little pieces of paper that she would puzzle over and try to give to us, as if conveying something immeasurably precious.

Because she was so disruptive she could be noisy, so was banned from the Chapter Room, particularly if there was someone giving a talk or lecture. We used to wonder what sort of mayhem would ensue if we could get her in for the Chapter of Faults, but we never managed it.

The novices entered the Chapter Room by a side entrance and Sister Pauline would stand plaintively watching us from a distance. We would smile at her and wave, and she would wave back excitedly. If Sister Mistress of Novices and Sister Marie-Germaine were not about, we would try to entice her by beckoning vigorously to her to join us. It was difficult to hide our glee if we succeeded. Because of her shuffling walk, we could always hear her coming and because the novices and postulants were seated nearest the door, we were aware of her imminent arrival before anyone else. She would burst in and look around with an air that combined triumph and determination. Reverend Mother General, seated majestically in the choir stall on the dais at the end of the room, could do nothing but glare at her.

Sister Pauline became rowdy when constrained. Out would come the little bits of paper, sometimes odd objects that she had purloined, a little mirror into which she stared earnestly and with which she began a loud if incomprehensible conversation. She was certainly disruptive, although most of the speakers were very tolerant. She absolutely adored the chaplain. If she had managed to break through the cordon that tried to prevent her from getting into the Chapter Room, and it was him giving the talk, she would shuffle rapidly down the room to sit as near to him as possible, listening rapt and silent until he had finished. One of the sisters tried gently to remove her once, but she set up such a howl of protest that the chaplain intervened, saying, "Let her stay; she does no harm." So she sat down again with a smirk of satisfaction.

In those days nobody used labels like dementia or Alzheimer's. Sister Pauline had "lost her mind", "was not herself", or, the best euphemism of all, "was very tired". Actually her energy was boundless and she almost always seemed happy, although I saw her crying once, head hanging like an unhappy child, because someone had scolded her. She died suddenly and unexpectedly.

"Sad," said Sister Marie-Germaine. "She didn't receive the Last Rites."

Very true, I thought, but she was spared the presence of Reverend Mother General sobbing at her bedside.

The day of her funeral was cold and dark, a heavy sky predicting rain. If the weather was very bad, the community just accompanied the coffin to the main door and left the pall-bearers to make their sad little journey on their own. We would then return to the chapel and recite the prayers of committal.

Apart from us getting wet, the real reason for avoiding the rain was the damage it did to the red fore-edges of the extremely expensive choir books. But in this instance, though bitterly cold, it was not raining, so we set off along the terrace. Halfway along, something fell on my hand and, looking up, I saw it was snowing. By the time we reached the end of the terrace, it was falling heavily. Sister Pauline would have relished the confusion that followed. Sister Marie-Suzanne, desperately anxious about the books, left her place at the back of the choir and hurried along the ranks, whispering agitatedly, "Cover the books, cover the books."

Reverend Mother General, indecisive, hesitated and then came to a virtual standstill, obviously wondering whether we should turn back. As we all had our heads down, our books enveloped in our cloaks, trying to follow the music, sing, and safeguard the precious edges, we all began to bump into each other, while the coffin continued independently ahead of us. Reverend Mother General, obviously feeling we might as well continue, then set off again at a brisk pace. We all hurried after her, with repeated and increasingly anguished whispers from Sister Marie-Suzanne on the one side, and "Keep up, keep up" from Sister Marie-Germaine on the other.

"Sister Pauline would love this," said Sister Odette in my ear.

"What, this shambles?"

"Well, yes, that too, but the snow. She loved the snow."

Then I remembered once seeing her in the cloister garden when I was dusting inside. She was turning dreamily in a circle, her arms outstretched, the snow falling on her face, her mouth open to catch the flakes, apparently oblivious to the cold. Her reverie was interrupted brusquely by a passing sister and she was brought gently indoors, protesting all the while.

We missed her. She had brought an innocent and harmless distraction to us and perhaps we gave her some pleasure, filling her lost world with memories of youth. I hope so. Otherwise, thoughtlessly and selfishly, we were just exploiting and teasing a bewildered old lady for our own amusement. It was one or the other, but I hope the former.

CHAPTER 17

The Turkey Experience

As postulants we had been spared the rigours of the annual spring-cleaning, known as "*le grand ménage*", but from the beginning of Lent, each Wednesday and Friday, we took off our habits after breakfast, dressed in our black overalls, and set to. We did two or three rooms a week, beginning in the attic and moving down through the house. Nothing escaped. Cleaning the attic was a filthy job; dust and grime, which had dropped down from the rafters together with cobwebs and what looked like mice droppings, covered everything.

"This is all going to be done again next year. What is the point of this? The attic is just an attic where things we don't need are stored."

"I shouldn't start complaining yet," said Sister Odette. "There's a long way to go before we get to the cellar."

We didn't actually do the cellar, but it wouldn't have surprised me if we had. In the rest of the house, the task was even more intense. Almost everything that could be removed from a room was taken out in order to have literally a clean sweep. This clichéd terminology had some meaning. Mattresses, pillows, blankets, and curtains were beaten and aired. Cupboards, drawers, tables, and chairs were polished.

The floors, whether wooden or tiled, were the big task and consequently several of us were needed to attack them. The parquet was scrubbed to remove every vestige of old polish and then the new polish was applied. It was fearsome semi-liquid stuff, smelling strongly but not unpleasantly of lavender and turpentine.

It was savage on the hands. The cloths we put it on with had to be disposed of with great care. I was told they would burst into flame if left bundled up together in a warm place. They certainly made my hands feel as if they were likely to be subjected to the unlikely phenomenon of spontaneous combustion.

The tiled floors were easier to deal with, as in the main they were just scrubbed, but one or two had to be polished with a lurid red lotion. This, although considerably kinder on the skin, left our hands looking as blood-stained as Lady Macbeth's for several days. This level of spring cleaning seemed quite normal to the French novices and was apparently an annual feature in their own homes.

It is a myth to believe that the working class, in France at any rate, don't know how to keep themselves clean. Any house that I've ever been into in France, owned or rented by ordinary working people, has been immaculate. It is usually the middle or upper classes who are prepared to put up with a degree of squalor that would be unacceptable to any respectable working-class French housewife. A young French woman told me that the first thing she did on getting home after buying a new article of clothing was to wash it or send it to the cleaners.

"Good God," she said, when I expressed astonishment. "Think of the number of people who might have tried it on."

Lent passed calmly. One Friday, instead of the *grand ménage*, we were told that Sister Bernadette, always smilingly cheerful in her wellingtons on farm or garden work, needed help plucking turkeys for the Easter celebration. Sister Susan was excused on the grounds of her phobia. It was bitterly cold, the ground rock hard, and the wind icy. We trooped down to the farmyard and were installed in a low stone shed with benches around the walls, where we could be a little protected from the wind.

The yard was full of turkeys. I was seated near the entrance, so had an excellent view of what happened next. Sister Bernadette grabbed a bird and, tucking it expertly under her arm, bound its legs with twine and hung it up on a pole suspended between two strong hooks. With a small and obviously very sharp knife, she cut its throat. It made no noise at all, but as the blood dripped onto the stone beneath, its wings fell open very slowly and in the wind it rotated gently on the string. Then she grabbed the next one.

Gruesomely, the remaining turkeys, not only oblivious to the fate of their fellows but ignorant of their own, relished pecking cheerfully at the blood dripping and freezing in the cold as it fell. Several turkeys were dispatched with amazing speed and when they had stopped bleeding, each of us received one, flung across our laps together with a hessian sack for the feathers.

It was not unpleasant; quite the contrary. The cold was so biting that having a large warm corpse on the knee was comforting.

Sister Annie shuddered and began to pluck, daintily holding each individual feather fastidiously between finger and thumb. Kind Sister Paule showed us the knack.

"Grasp a little bunch of feathers and grip them against the heel of your thumb. You should pull in the direction that the feathers lie, otherwise you might tear the skin; though it is less likely as the bird is still warm."

"Warm! This one's heart is still beating!" said Sister Thérèse, snorting nervously. "Any minute now it's going to turn its head and peck me."

Poor Sister Annie let out such a yelp of horror that even stern Odette relented and soothed her, assuring her it was just a joke.

A five-kilo turkey takes a lot of plucking and only the skilled among us could do one in less than an hour and a half. It was a new occupation for most of us and we were prepared to enjoy it. We sat in a snowy swirling haze of feathers, sneezing often, the air filled with the pungent odour of bird faeces.

At about 11:00 a.m., Sister Bernadette called a halt and we stumbled outside. A sister from the kitchen trundled a flat wooden barrow into the yard and uncovered a basket full of large slices of bread and jam. There was also an enormous chipped jug of hot sweet white wine with toasted bread floating in it. The effects were instant, and we were flooded with warmth. The alcohol content was minimal, as it had been boiled off, but the drink was delicious and invigorating. We devoured the bread and jam with filthy hands and shared the mugs.

We returned at the end of the morning and, in the warmth of Sacré-Coeur, took off our blue aprons. Looking down at my overall, I saw a curious grey stain that covered the whole of the front. On closer inspection, I saw that this was a moving mass of mites. My gasp of horror was echoed by the others as they discovered the same thing. We were infested. A determined crocodile of them was moving across Sister Odette's bandeau and, as Sister Paule moved her head, I saw her veil was alive with them. We were seized with a communal panic and began to cry out in revulsion.

"To the showers immediately!"

Sister Marie-Suzanne's directive was obeyed instantly. We raced noisily up the stairs, meeting Sister Mistress of Novices on the landing, come out to see what the rumpus was about.

In the shower room we shed our clothes with frantic haste. No strippers ever divested themselves of their clothes more rapidly than we did. We shrieked as each article of clothing revealed more and more of our unwelcome guests, and shot naked into the showers, two at a time, indifferent to our nudity. Sister Mistress of Novices arrived with a drum of white powder that I assume was some form of DDT and sprinkled it liberally over our divested garments and then, for good measure, over us. We arrived in the refectory a little late for dinner, our clothes went in a sack to the laundry and returned two days later, purged and immaculate.

We dreaded the next episode of turkey plucking just before Easter. Confident that we would receive a lot of sympathy on our return, we were prepared to enjoy the same vocal exclamations of disgust and the same excitement, but were pulled up short by Sister Marie-Suzanne. She had the showers, the DDT, and clean clothes ready for us. At the first outburst, she froze us into silence.

"That's enough! Stop immediately! Sister Mistress of Novices wants me to say to you that this inconvenience is a very small thing to put up with compared to what our Blessed Saviour Jesus Christ suffered on the cross for you!"

There's not a lot you can say to that. We smiled sheepishly at each other, went quietly and meekly upstairs, and showered with decorum.

The week before Easter Sunday was both dramatic and depressing. All the bells were silenced and we were summoned to prayer, to eat, and to play by a harsh wooden rattle. In Sacré-Coeur we were called to order by a clapper. During the day, although disconcerting, the noise was at least expected, but to be woken at 5:30 a.m. by this uncompromisingly brutal clatter was unpleasant and even alarming. The depressing atmosphere was further compounded by the particularly foul weather following the icy spell, which meant that we were confined to the Noviciate, even for recreation.

On Holy Saturday the house fell silent. There was no evening recreation and we went to bed immediately after supper. Sleep was brief, if indeed we managed it. We rose at 11:30 p.m. and on the stroke of midnight filed into the chapel. It looked magnificent, the altar cloths white and gold. Sister Marie-Suzanne on the dais in front of the choir steadied us with her raised hand and then we began the great liturgy of Easter. It was powerful, emotional, magnificent, uplifting, and terribly tiring. We were back in bed by 3:00 a.m. and up again to the familiar sound of the bell at 7:00 a.m. for Laudes, meditation, breakfast with brioche, and High Mass at 10:00 a.m. After the grim week behind us, we were charmed to find the weather had changed. It was still cold but sunny and after dinner we escaped into the charmilles and ran like animals let out from their winter confinement.

It was about that time that a blood donor unit came to the town and we were all asked if we would like to volunteer. A little bus came to pick us up and we drove for fifteen minutes or so to the unit. The only building in the area with a large enough reception area to accommodate stretchers and all the paraphernalia was the reception area of the local abattoir. We thought this gruesome but hilarious and so arrived, not in a serious "I am here to do my civic duty" mode, but in ribald disarray. The sight of the donors' blood dripping into bottles suspended from the stretchers made me queasy. I did donate blood, although with some unease.

In May, the postulants were "clothed" and joined us in Sacré-Coeur, and a week or so later the second-year novices made their profession, received their "obedience" and departed. We were sad to see them go. These were women with whom we had lived in intimacy for a year. It also reduced our number; we were now only thirteen in all.

We didn't know it at the time, but there was already a serious problem of recruitment, not just for the Sisters of Evron but for most religious congregations, both male and female. When I entered the Noviciate, there were about twenty novices and our arrival meant a 50 per cent increase. The reduction in numbers in the house after a profession was compensated by the arrival of new novices. But following the "clothing" of our English postulant, rosy-cheeked Sister Clare, and her companions, there were no new entrants the following November and from then on postulants only arrived in very small numbers and infrequently. This dearth of new recruits was a catastrophe. With no young nuns to replace the old, the congregation would get smaller and over time it would mean some establishments would have to be closed. In some other areas the workforce would be spread very thinly; one nun might have to take on work previously done by three. If the trend continued, the 300-year-old institution would inevitably die.

However, there was another element that compounded the situation. Few women were coming in, but an alarming number were also leaving, mainly the young professed nuns, probably for the same reason. Catholic laywomen were being given a vastly more positive role in day-to-day church activity. Marriage itself was being spoken of as a holy vocation and not a second-best option. The view that people married because they could not control their lust degraded marriage, so St Paul's admonition that it was better "to marry than to burn" was viewed, if not with opprobrium, then certainly with distaste.

CHAPTER 18

A "Hustings" and the Delights of Literature

In the spring of 1963 preparations were begun to call a General Chapter. This six-yearly event was to elect a Reverend Mother General and to deal with spiritual, administrative, and financial matters in the congregation. It was anticipated that in the light of the discussions that had taken place during the Vatican Council, there would be serious issues of adaptation and modification to be addressed. All convents had to elect delegates. Little convents grouped together until they had a quorum. In a big community like the Mother House there were several to be elected. Certain non-elected nuns could be invited to the Chapter because of a particular expertise, perhaps in the nursing or teaching field. It all seemed very organized and democratic. When I commented on this to Sister Marie-Suzanne, she raised her eyebrows. Her response was cryptic: "We must suppose so; we must hope so."

Her cynicism was justified. The mistrust of Sister Mistress of Novices, felt by some sisters in the Mother House, we hoped would be balanced by others who recognized her many qualities. Both sides canvassed enthusiastically for their preferred delegates.

In the Noviciate, we expected that either Sister Mistress of Novices or Sister Marie-Suzanne, or indeed both, would be elected as a delegate or invited to attend in an advisory capacity, as was the custom. On the day of the election, Sister Mistress of Novices and Sister Marie-Suzanne set off promptly.

"Well, which one is it?" somebody asked eagerly when they returned a few hours later. They looked at each other and smiled thinly.

"It's neither one nor the other." Sister Mistress of Novices spoke cheerfully but she was flushed and, I suspect, not a little angry. Sister Marie-Suzanne was tight-lipped.

"What!" We were dumbfounded.

"Well," she continued, "we are not required. Obviously, if they need us, we will be happy to offer advice if and when it is asked for."

We tried to pump her for information at recreation.

"But you'll go as a consultant?"

"It seems not."

After that the subject was closed. By the next day she had regained her composure and was her usual slightly ironic self. She never referred to it again.

That episode was more than a snub; it was an insult and I am sure she felt it deeply. It was also very short-sighted. She was responsible for the formation of the candidates aspiring to the religious life, and clearly had some experience and input to offer. To have a General Chapter to discuss renewal and adaptation to the twentieth century and not to take her opinion into account was clearly absurd.

We knew the Rule would be reviewed. The Vatican Council had asked all religious congregations to consider their initial foundation and spirituality and to return to the fundamentals as much as possible. Depressingly, there was much talk of changing our habit, as if by looking at the external symbols we were addressing the important issues. Many of us felt it should be left as it was for the time being or abandoned all together. We had seen some of the new "modernized" habits of other congregations and thought them uniformly hideous and pointless.

The religious habit had become a curious hybrid. Originally it was the dress of the period, as any picture of working men and women from medieval times until the early nineteenth century shows. The coif of the Sisters of La Retraite was identical to the headdress worn by Catherine of Aragon, wife of Henry VIII. Then, around the beginning of the eighteenth century, gradually the habit began to assume a life and significance of its own so that even when women's heads were no longer covered and skirts got shorter, the habit still maintained a symbolic dimension. The nun was visible because of her appearance, and the different forms and colours began to identify the different congregations and orders. The best that could be said about the habit was that it was picturesque, elegant even, but in terms of hygiene it was problematic, and proud though I was to wear it, the whole thing was dreadfully impractical and in the twentieth century an anachronism.

The election of the delegates was, for the Noviciate, a week's excitement and then we mostly forgot about it. What was foremost in our minds at that time was how we were to incorporate the external activity that we were allowed, as second-year novices, into our cloistered life. Once the canonical year was completed, we were permitted to work a limited number of hours in a capacity that allowed us to exercise our abilities or talents, such as they were, and to prepare us for our lives when we would be professed nuns.

My sister novices were duly employed in and around the Mother House. Sister Agnès went to help in the kitchen, Sister Odette to the domestic science school Ma Maison, Sister Annie to the secretariat, and the others to work in the parish or at the primary school. Sister Susan, a musician, became responsible for the organ music that was a part of the Sunday and feast day ceremonial. She didn't know how to play the organ, although her knowledge of the piano undoubtedly helped. She took instruction from the elderly sister whose arthritis was making this too hard a task.

And this left me. It was clear that as I had no qualifications and no apparent ability, they didn't know what to do with me at all. One morning Sister Mistress of Novices sent for me.

"What we thought," she announced cheerfully, "was that you

should follow a course of study in French literature; the one that the pupils at St Julien and Notre Dame in Le Mans are doing for their *baccalauréat*. I am sure that you will love it."

I did love reading the books and the commentaries. I completed all the written exercises, supremely confident of the quality of my work, as initially I had no one to correct or to criticize them. Sister Marie-Suzanne did her best, saying diffidently that it wasn't really her field of expertise. Sister Mistress of Novices was always too busy, though on one occasion when Sister Marie-Suzanne passed her a criticism of Corneille's *Cinna* that I had done after a visit to the theatre, she asked me, "Where did you get this from?"

"From my head," I replied, surprised.

She just nodded and went away. The next day she presented me with a copy of *Andromache*, saying, "Let's see what you can do with that." She took it when I had completed the essay and said vaguely that she would get it looked at.

About a week later it came back, covered in red pen. My work had been passed to the headmistress of St Julien, a nun of terrifying intellect, who, later on, I was to get to know much better. I thought I'd done quite a reasonable job, so was stunned by her comments. My work had no "form". The French have a rigid format for essays, and students who try for something more spontaneous, less structured, are marked down, no matter how good their arguments. For an English girl, even one as badly educated as I was, this was very alien and I was quite ready to argue the point. Up until this time I had been working away happily with no one to criticize my efforts, so was taken aback.

"It is very good for you." Sister Mistress of Novices was sympathetic but intransigent. "Sister Margaret-Marie has offered to continue to correct your work and even to set you some and you will follow her advice. Anyway, we all know it is true. You *are* far too emotional. You must learn to be more detached in everything. Forgetfulness of self, that's the key. You are not here for *you*; no matter what work you do, you do it for him. You are here for God."

So I learned the dry format of essay writing, and certainly it concentrated my mind and discouraged rambling. But there were some wonderful occasions – trips to the theatre and a marvellous series of lectures, given by the acerbic Jesuit we had met when we were postulants, on notable French writers of the late nineteenth and twentieth centuries: Charles Péguy, Paul Claudel, Georges Bernanos, Paul Éluard, Louis Aragon, and Jacques Maritain, among others. Our lecturer-priest, radical misogynist that he was and anti-nun to boot, refused to let us sit in the amphitheatre.

"No bonnets in the hall," he declared, seeming to believe that the presence of nuns would inhibit questions from the floor. So I sat in the wings, but my appreciation of his talks was not diminished by being stuffed in a corner. I drank it all in.

It was noticeable that with the external activity in which we were involved, our recreational conversations were wider. We were discouraged from talking about ourselves. This was viewed as selfish, as those of a less outgoing temperament tended to remain silent, and recreation was supposed to give everyone a chance to relax and talk. But with a broader field of activity, we listened to pleasant anecdotes and innocent gossip about the Mother House and elsewhere. My companions, with a total lack of envy, shared my enjoyment of the theatre and the lectures. We were reasonably enough discouraged from making ourselves the centre of these stories, something I found very hard. I had come to realize during my time in community that I was very full of myself, a natural show-off. All through my life it's got me into trouble.

The Noviciate was further enlivened by the arrival of second-year novices from Lisdoonvarna, the English-speaking Noviciate. They came to France for four months to help them to appreciate the Frenchness and spirituality of the congregation. Sister Susan had visited the Mother House before she entered the convent and requested exceptionally to do her own noviciate in France rather in Ireland. It was just pure luck on my part that the next candidate who presented herself was me and I was roped in so that Sister Susan would not be the only English novice. Given that we were barred almost immediately from speaking English together I don't think it made much difference to her. The Lisdoonvarna novices claimed that their own training was far stricter than ours and they were astonished by the easy teasing communication we had with all our mistresses.

Once, in St Anne, they listened with horror to an exchange between Sister Eugenie and Sister Clare.

"This will all have to be unpicked and redone. Your hem's too wide; I said a *good* centimetre."

Sister Clare looked mutinous. "It's either a centimetre or it's not a centimetre. I don't know what a good centimetre is."

"A good centimetre is just a tiny bit more than a centimetre. This is nearly a centimetre and a half."

"So you mean a centimetre and a quarter."

"No, I don't I mean a centimetre and a quarter. I mean a *good* centimetre."

Sister Clare retired muttering under her breath. The Irish novices gave me to understand that they wouldn't have dared to answer back like that. It would probably have earned them more than a reproof – they would have eaten their supper while kneeling, perhaps. I wasn't quite sure if they were joking or not.

Despite their apparently more severe training, they were a friendly, lively group. One of them, Sister Catriona, had been a county champion Irish dancer. Sister Mistress of Novices would get her to perform for us sometimes, and even without music we were riveted by her tapping feet. I had never seen Irish dancing before and was not particularly impressed by the stiff arms held at the side, as I was used to the "antler" arms of Scottish reels, but the footwork and the high knees, even when the latter were hidden by a habit, were extraordinarily dynamic. Sister Catriona was a tall, nervous, ungainly girl with a pretty pointed face, but when she danced she was transformed.

CHAPTER 19

A Sawdust Carpet and a Private Epiphany

One of the church's annual feast days that most involved the Noviciate was Corpus Christi, known in France as *la Fête-Dieu*. In non-Catholic countries, it is usually celebrated on a Sunday, as it involves a solemn procession, quite often of some distance on public roads, and can seriously disrupt week-day traffic and lead to heated exchanges between participants and motorists not in keeping with the spirit of the occasion. The custom is to prepare a carpet for the passage of the Holy Eucharist and this is most commonly of flowers.

The preparations began the day before the feast. It was always a worrying time for the organizers, the vagaries of the weather being what they were. Choosing late spring or early summer for this event had been, I thought, very sensible, as the chances were, particularly in warmer climes, that God would smile on our efforts and at least hold off the rain. I do remember occasions in England when we were not so fortunate and the parishioners were reduced to following the Blessed Sacrament round and round inside the church, as the rain lashed pitilessly down outside, washing away the beautiful carpet of flowers so lovingly prepared the previous day. God, I sometimes feel, has a very odd sense of humour! His tendency to put a spoke in the wheel is well recognized.

A story is told of the great St Teresa of Avila, the reforming Spanish Carmelite nun. In the course of a journey to visit a distant convent, her covered cart was thrown on its side when crossing a rocky river-bed. She suffered a broken arm and severe bruising. Rather crossly she reproached God, saying, "Why have you allowed this? Am I not going about your work?"

God replied, "Teresa, my daughter, I treat all my friends this way."

Quick as a flash she replied, "No wonder you've got so few of them!"

So although I am not a great one for thinking that he ought to intervene in day-to-day events, believing that we were given the ability to sort out our own mess, I do think that it wouldn't have been too seismic an event to have laid on a bit of sunshine; but in any event France was sunny for both the feasts of Corpus Christi during my time as a novice.

Sister Marie-Suzanne assembled us before we set off to lay the "carpet" in the charmilles and stressed that this task, although "not easy", was to be done to the very best of our ability, as we were preparing it for Our Lord. I was puzzled, thinking it wasn't too taxing to scatter a few flower heads and rose-petals. I was even more puzzled when we were issued with small trowels.

We trooped out and found the alleys marked out in three bands. At regular intervals all along were small heaps, not of flower heads, but of red and green coloured sawdust. It was, as Sister Marie-Suzanne said, "not easy". We were not preparing a rose-petal path.

The sawdust was sticky and surprisingly difficult to spread smoothly. We had to keep within the lines, using the tools that we had been issued with, to tidy up the edge of the broad red band, before filling the outer borders with green. Doing this for a protracted time on hands and knees was hard work, and not for the first time I was grateful for the corset. We were like a troupe of pavement artists but without the variety.

It was monotonous work, took all day to complete, and was often frustrating, as frequently there were areas that had to be repaired. Although the sawdust was damp, it was easily disturbed by a variety of things. Reverend Mother General and several other sisters, coming to assess the progress, inadvertently caused havoc with their hems.

"She might have brought chocolates," grumbled Sister Odette crossly, repairing the damage.

The odd pigeon dropping down and wandering along the central path was the least of our problems, for they could be shooed away, but the wind, even a gentle breeze, could interrupt the perfect edge and, if the red and the green became mixed, the whole area had to be scraped clean and redone, or it looked muddy and indistinct. Periodically we went to see how the other carpet layers were getting on and to admire their progress. At the beginning of the day, we were meticulous in our work, and we were also fresh. By early afternoon, the length still to be completed seemed endless and we were dead tired, with aching backs and sore hands. Sawdust is abrasive material.

We were encouraged in our endeavours by both Sister Mistress of Novices and Sister Marie-Suzanne, who passed by periodically to see how we were getting on. The form this encouragement took was radically different: the former saying, "Do it beautifully, beautifully; it's for Christ's own passage among us," while the latter exhorted: "Hurry up, hurry up; just get it down reasonably neatly. We've to be finished by Vespers. We've only got another hour." It was completed on time.

Early the following morning after breakfast we went to tidy up any overnight damage. The "carpet" looked amazingly good, but by the time priests, acolytes, townspeople, and community had passed along it, nothing was left except a scuffed and indistinct mess. I was very relieved to discover that we were not going to be called on to scoop it all up afterwards. This was a job for the workmen. The thought of another day on hands and knees was a daunting one.

We were often involved in tasks that put us on our hands and knees. The rough, opaque cider that we drank at all meals, except breakfast, came from a local cooperative to which the Mother

House contributed. The apples were harvested in late autumn when all the leaves had fallen, and the round brightly coloured fruit hung on the trees like Christmas baubles. A workman, using a stout forked pole, shook the apples down so that they fell in a circle around the trunk. Gathering them was a disagreeable job. We knelt around the trees, our petticoats and stockings soaking up the dew like sponges. The grass was long and wet, and the apples small, so it was a matter of scratching around for them. The slugs found them sooner than we did, so small grey molluscs often found their way into the large collection baskets.

"I hope these are going to be washed before they go to the press," I said.

"Probably not," Sister Agnès replied cheerfully. "There's a lot more apple than slug, and anyway they'll all be killed off by the fermentation."

"That's what I am afraid of; slug cider doesn't appeal to me." I thought again about the bits floating in the bottles, which were sometimes quite substantial. I was no longer reassured that they were just bits of apple. It was yet another "black pudding" moment.

That second summer as a novice was the usual busy round of retreats and conferences. I was calmer and more at peace with myself. Life was organized and the routine steadied my restlessness and impetuosity; I was deeply happy.

One hot afternoon during our annual retreat, having found a gap in the hornbeam hedge, I crept into the orchard, sat down, and settled myself comfortably on the ground, my back against a tree. It was very quiet and I was very hot. In a kind of sleepy detachment, I began to take off my shoes and stockings, and wriggled my bare feet in the warm grass. I was reading about Charles de Foucauld, whose youth of rakish dissipation as an army officer was transformed by his discovery of Christ. I was meditating on a sentence from his biography: "My God, if you exist, let me come to know you."

I said the words over and over to myself and fell into a sort of reverie. I felt suspended, weightless, and lost all sense of time and place. Under my toes, the soil was warm and I was overwhelmed with a deep and wonderful tranquillity, a certainty that I was in God's presence, and that he knew me and loved me. The moment was all-encompassing. I felt flooded with light.

The bell for Vespers sounded distant and I was only aware that it had rung when it stopped. Still dazed, I walked slowly back to the Noviciate. It seemed quite unimportant that I was missing an Office and slow to obey the summons of the bell. I barely felt the path and was oblivious to the fact that I was barefooted. In the cool dim hall, I met Sister Marie-Suzanne, who had noted my absence: she never missed anything. She opened her mouth to reprimand me but presumably something in my face stopped her. Her eyes fell to my feet.

"Where are your shoes and stockings?"

I looked down at my bare feet. "I must have left them in the charmilles." I still felt stunned.

"You'd better go back and fetch them. Wait, I'll come with you." Perhaps she thought I didn't look fit to go anywhere by myself.

We walked in silence to the gap in the hedge where I had squeezed through to find my isolated spot, and picked up my abandoned things. Typically she frowned and tut-tutted as my veil caught momentarily on a twig.

"What are you reading?" she asked, taking the book from my hand.

"A life of Charles de Foucauld."

"You could do worse than imitate him, though I don't recommend that you take your shoes and stockings off in order to do so, nor that you ignore the bell *and* miss Vespers." Her slight smile belied the strictness of her voice.

The wonderful enlightened moment that I experienced that hot and sunny afternoon was never repeated, although I yearned for it, so it remains with me just a privileged memory. If it was the sun and autosuggestion, I ought to have been able to recreate that dazzling moment. Sadly I was not, although, God knows, I tried often enough.

At my monthly meeting for spiritual direction with Sister Mistress of Novices, I tried, haltingly, to tell her about it, but it sounded banal, even trivial, and I realized that although she listened encouragingly, it had no meaning for her. It was my personal experience, my epiphany.

"You never know when you're going to meet God," she mused when I had finished explaining. "Of course he is there all the time; it is just that we often don't notice. You must learn to love yourself, to value yourself. I don't mean that you can just coast, and it's not a question of trying harder; it's to do with being open to the Holy Spirit and listening with your heart. Don't forget that for God you are priceless, his own marvellous creature." She laughed. "You've got a lot to live up to."

At the end of summer, my parents came to visit me again, bringing my brother. My delight at seeing them was tempered by my concern at my mother's appearance. She was dreadfully thin and nervously restless. My father said she was totally dependent on the tablets she was taking, which she seemed to swallow by the handful. Nobody at that time was aware of the addictive nature of the amphetamines that had been prescribed for her in an effort to alleviate the effects of her chronic insomnia. The theory was: if she can't sleep, let's make her feel better during the day.

My father told me that initially the result had been wonderful; full of energy, she seemed to enjoy life to the full. Gradually, this energy became frenetic activity and she was incapable of rest or relaxation, becoming alternately obsessive or depressed. She put on quite a good show for me, but beneath her delight at seeing me, I sensed a deep sadness. They had planned a few extra days down on the Loire, but my mother ran out of her tablets, and as they were only available on prescription, she was unable to get more. The rest of the holiday was a nightmare for all three of them.

Despite my worry, there were light moments. My brother, Peter, who had become truly handsome in the two years since I had last seen him, showed Sister Mistress of Novices "the twist" and answered her queries about the Beatles. She laughed delightedly at the absurdity of it. I asked him about our mother when I could get him alone for a moment, but he was only sixteen and was not in a position to tell me anything about her state of health or indeed about the state of our parents' marriage, which, I began to suspect, was the real cause of it all. I wept when they left.

I was haunted by my mother's wan and twitchy face and poured out my concern some days later to Sister Odette when we were washing our hair. We were supposed to keep the silence during this activity but I am afraid we often used the occasion to discuss things that we felt we couldn't talk about at recreation. She listened thoughtfully to my expressions of anguish and anxiety, and pointed out very reasonably that, even if I were at home, in all probability there would be nothing I could do.

A nun is expected to put her family and its concerns very much into second place, if not actually to sideline them. She has left the world and its considerations behind her; that's the theory. In practice this is often very difficult and I was extremely fortunate to have the sympathy not only of Sister Mistress of Novices but also of Reverend Mother General, who gave me permission to write home once a fortnight. The Rule allowed only a monthly letter, so this was a great concession. After a while I became, if not less anxious, less acutely concerned as the memory of her haggard face faded a little. My father had told me that they would not be able to come for my profession the following May, so I was resigned to not seeing them for some indeterminate period, and time and distance soothed me.

In January 1964 we, as second-year novices, began the serious preparation for our first vows in May. Vows are made initially for a specific period, known as temporal vows. Final vows are made with a view to a lifetime commitment. A nun in temporal vows is free to leave on the anniversary day of her vows should she wish, with no obligation on either side. If she wishes to leave while still bound by her temporal vows, in order to regularize things it is considered only polite, to say the least, to ask for a dispensation from them.

In our congregation, there were eight and a half years between the beginning of the postulancy and the taking of final vows: two and a half years as postulant and novice, and six years as a professed nun. We made vows annually for three years and then made a commitment for a period of three years. So after six years of temporal vows we could be admitted to final profession. It was not a rushed business!

The vows are a private commitment, made to God, within the framework of a given religious organization. They have no legal standing in secular society. No one can be constrained to remain in religious life against their will, although granting dispensation from final vows takes longer, as the application for dispensation has to go to Rome. The effect of this delay, and Rome is sometimes terribly slow, often means that a subject gets tired of waiting and leaves anyway. This causes consternation, for within the context of the Rule, they remain bound by the commitment. Every effort is made to contact the "renegade", serve the dispensation, and get it signed. It is not uncommon for a nun to ask to be released from her vows and, after some time in a secular environment, to request to return to her congregation or order. So nuns leaving after making final vows are offered a sort of cooling off period known as ex-claustration before their release is ratified. This allows them to return if they wish.

My second year as a novice passed so quickly that profession seemed to be on me almost unexpectedly. There was now not the slightest doubt in my mind that my commitment was absolute and that I was doing the right, indeed the only, possible thing. Even the "baggage" that had weighed so heavily throughout my postulancy and first year of the noviciate training seemed easy to carry. My only concern or uncertainty was about what was going to happen to me after profession. Would I stay in France or return to England?

The evening before we were due to go into retreat in preparation for our profession, Sister Mistress of Novices called us into her anteroom. We didn't notice until she spoke that some of our number were missing.

"Sister Annie and Sister Susan," she said, "have asked to delay their profession for six months."

I was stunned, aghast that Sister Susan, of whom I was so fond, would not make her profession with me. She had been with me since the beginning, tolerated my pretensions, and been so supportive. We had shared so much – including all those "black pudding" moments.

I looked at Sister Odette. She looked frozen in disbelief and as we left the room slow tears ran down her face.

"I don't mind too much about Sister Annie, but Sister Susan, dear Sister Susan, it's unthinkable."

"At least we were told beforehand – not like Sister Yvonne who disappeared without trace."

"You're right, but what can we say to her?"

"It was her choice, so we must say we are sorry but support her in her decision."

Which was what we did, but it saddened us none the less.

Our profession took place in the intimacy of the chapel rather than in the grandiose setting of the basilica, with only the community and the families of the professed present, and was a more sober but much more significant affair. I was sorry that my parents were not with me. I suddenly had a great yearning for my mother.

After breakfast we put on the new habits that we had made under the strict tutelage of Sisters Eugenie and Yvonne, and exchanged our white novice veil and the Peter Pan collar for the black veil and large white collar of the professed nun. Our profession followed High Mass; we were not excused choir duty even that day.

Placing our hands between those of Reverend Mother General, we pronounced our vows, reading carefully from a small white card held between our fingers. Over our neat black veils, she placed the long fine communion veil that hung to our hips, and pinned it on. We also received the small, exquisitely carved wooden crucifix that we would wear on our breast.

"I was born to love and serve you, my God," I prayed in my heart, thinking again of St Augustus. "You made us for yourself,

O Lord, and our hearts are restless till they rest in you." Then there was the Te Deum and I was finally a professed religious, a nun at last.

Back in Sacré-Coeur, Sister Mistress of Novices, with tender and smiling affection, unpinned our communion veils and helped us fold them.

"You never thought that I would make it, did you?" I asked Sister Marie-Suzanne that evening at recreation.

She laughed but she also blushed. "No, I didn't, but you have and I am very happy to have been proved wrong."

Our joy at being professed was attenuated not only by Sister Susan and Sister Annie, but also by the knowledge that our time together as novices was coming to an end.

We received our "obedience" a few days later. Reverend Mother General also expressed her surprise that I had made it to profession. I didn't know whether to take it as a compliment or an insult. Suddenly, like an afterthought, she said, "Tell me, when I came across you and Sister Annie in the cloister when you were still postulants. Do you remember, you were jumping and swinging your arms? What on earth were you doing?"

"We were dancing, Reverend Mother."

"Dancing! In the cloister! At that time in the morning! What on earth for?"

As I was at a loss to know what difference she thought the time made to our actions, I didn't reply. She continued to look bemused and was silent for a moment then, as if suddenly remembering the purpose of our meeting, said, "You will, of course, be returning to England eventually. Mother Henrietta, your Mother Provincial, not unreasonably wants her English subjects back, but not straight away. We are sending you for two or three months to St Julien, our school in Le Mans. Sister Superior would like you to help with English conversation for those pupils doing their *baccalauréat*."

My uncertainty was resolved and this news delighted me. I rushed back to the Noviciate.

"I'm going to St Julien!"

"Of course you are," said Sister Mistress of Novices, smiling broadly. I didn't know if she had engineered it, but once again I was aware of her partiality for me and was grateful.

Over the next few days, excitement and anticipation were mixed with real sadness as one by one my lovely companions left. Sister Superior, from the domestic science school Ma Maison, coming to collect Sister Odette who was returning there, saw my distress.

"Don't be sad. Nothing can separate loving hearts," she assured me. Those words were to comfort me for many years.

On the day of my departure, I hugged Sister Susan and thanked her for all her many kindnesses. Sister Mistress of Novices walked me through the town to the station, and with every step the lump in my throat got bigger. We stood in silence waiting for the train and, when it arrived, I could no longer contain my tears. I wept unashamedly, my nose streaming. She comforted me as best she could and wiped my eyes with her own handkerchief.

I watched out of the window until the train rounded the bend and I lost her to view. I didn't know it then, but I was not to see her again for over twenty-five years.

PART 3

Profession

CHAPTER 20

St Julien's School, Le Mans

I was welcomed to the school cheerfully, if hastily. Summer term is a busy time and I am sure the community had a lot more on their minds than organizing a timetable for me. So I was lucky that several of the sisters put themselves out to find a slot for me. The community was delightful, a group of easy-going, busy, committed women, and the four months I spent with them were very rewarding, but adaptation was difficult.

First, there were no bells for us: those that rang were electric and for the pupils. So I woke to an alarm clock in the small but bright bedroom that I had been given. I was alone, so there was no pious verbal ejaculation to galvanize me out of bed. What a temptation to turn over again for another five minutes!

The Mother House was the model for the spiritual life of the congregation. The Office and personal prayer dictated the day. It was very interesting to arrive at a school where the primary purpose was teaching, and to see how the Office and the spiritual life were accommodated. In retrospect I felt that we were ill-prepared in the Noviciate for this new autonomy.

We did have a community Mass and recited the Office together when we were free, but all this was fitted around the demands of the school. So a great deal of personal discipline was needed. After all, nobody would know if you had missed anything.

After some discussion with Sister Superior, it was decided that I should spend three hours a week in English conversation with the *baccalauréat* classes. It was left to me to decide what the topics should be. I had absolutely no experience in this sort of thing and was very apprehensive, as the girls were only about three years younger than me. I had them in small groups and they were friendly, polite, and interested. It was easier than I expected; I asked them about their lives, their families, and their expectations, and they asked me about the Royal Family, with whom they were fascinated. Princess Margaret was their favourite; they actually knew far more about her than I did.

From the library, I acquired several books by Agatha Christie, who was extremely popular in France, then as now. I got the pupils to read passages aloud, correcting their pronunciation. I would ask them to explain the plot or to describe a character. Sometimes, because the group was small, we sat outside.

Pleasant as all this was, however, it was hardly enough to keep me fully occupied, so I asked Sister Superior if I could sit in on some art classes. The art teacher was a nun of exceptional talent who exhibited her work both locally and nationally, and one of her classes was Art Appreciation.

"I have to teach painting and drawing. It's dreadfully boring," she confided. "I'd much prefer to talk about great art and great painting."

Her taste was eclectic. She was devoted to the fifteenth-century masters, and taught me to love the little po-faced Virgin Mary with her sumptuous robes seated in improbable bucolic landscapes, the angels with multi-coloured wings, the stylized and symbolic gardens. But she was equally passionate about Rubens, Rembrandt, Hieronymus Bosch, and on down the centuries to Braque and Picasso. She would talk enthusiastically about any of them. From her I learned that a distinction must be made, when looking at a painting, between *joli*, *gentil*, and *beau*.

"There is plenty of art," she pointed out, "that can be described as *pretty*. Sometimes the subject matter can be said to be *nice, pretty* and *nice*, like the Impressionists, some of whose work is also *beautiful*." This was a concession: she wasn't a big fan. "But there is some art that is neither pretty nor nice but *is* beautiful. Beauty is creative for the artist *and* for the observer. It touches the heart and the soul, not just our sentiments. It changes the way we look at the world and our perceptions of things. It gives us an insight and even an understanding of the world about us." She cited, as examples, Grunewald's *Crucifixion*, with Christ's lacerated, distorted, and tormented body, and Picasso's *Guernica*, all howling grief and outrage, nothing pretty or nice there.

When she was involved in preparing for an exhibition, she would arrive in the refectory with her hands covered in oils, her gaze distant. She was clearly somewhere else.

"She's lost in a world of paint and turpentine, her mind filled with form and colour."The headmistress Sister Marguerite-Marie's observation was as shrewd as it was affectionate. "Thank God she's not the cook!"

I was still submitting work for Sister Marguerite-Marie, who had first evaluated my amateurish attempts at critical analysis when I was a novice. She was known to her *baccalauréat* classes as "Madame Mère", Napoleon's affectionate but respectful nickname for his mother. Her pupils adored her. Small and slight, full of energy with a bouncing walk, she never sat down in the classroom but strolled up and down, her hands in her pockets and her sharp pointed little nose in the air. She was very demanding, expecting hard work and total commitment. She wanted "serious students", but her wit and easy charm more than made up for her sometimes acerbic tongue. A few in the community were uneasy with her, finding her brusque and sometimes unapproachable. Some felt she was an intellectual snob, and she *was* contemptuous of intellectual laziness, which she thought a sin against the Holy Ghost.

She too was subject to moments of distraction. On one occasion, going to the cathedral for High Mass, her missal tucked under her arm, her mind no doubt filled with some knotty philosophical problem, she arrived at the great door only to discover that the object under her arm was not, in fact, her missal but her alarm clock.

"It wasn't much help for the Mass," she said chuckling, "but it did allow me to know that one of the dreariest sermons I'd heard for a long time was overrunning by a good ten minutes and that I was going to be late for dinner. I seriously considered setting it off."

She gave me a lot of her time and was as generous with her praise as she was exigent with her expectations, insisting that I read some Proust. She told me that my like or dislike of him was "immaterial: it is his beautiful style that matters".

I should have known by her colouring that she was red-headed but this was unexpectedly revealed when, one hot evening at recreation, she took off her veil and bandeau and ran her hands vigorously through her hair. I am sure my own mouth dropped open with astonishment, but nobody else as much as blinked. For many of the older teaching nuns, the religious costume, the habit, was not very important. In the late nineteenth century, the French education system was secularized, and male and female religious were banned from teaching in schools. The sisters simply took off their habit, called themselves Mademoiselle or Madame, and carried on. So uncovering one's head was no big deal. They only began to wear the habit again in schools just before the Second World War. "Marshal Petain," I was told, "gave us back our habits." He was the reactionary president during the war years, but for some of the nuns, being allowed to wear their habit again was enough for them to overlook his nationalism, his anti-Semitism, his fascism, and his collaboration.

The community was the liveliest of any that I was to live in. The Rule seemed less an absolute than a framework that could be adapted not just to circumstances but to people if need be. An example was our personal correspondence. I submitted my letter home to Sister Superior, open as usual.

"Oh, seal it up," she said impatiently. "I have neither the time nor the inclination to read what you write to your family."

The community tended to treat her with affection rather than deference. She had an extraordinarily volatile temperament, her moods unpredictable, and although she was usually brisk, competent, and fair, she could also be moody and astonishingly bad-tempered. Occasionally she would arrive at mealtimes or recreation scowling ferociously and biting her fingers, sullenly silent or ready to pick a fight with anybody. The community knew better than to attempt to jolly her up.

Sister Marguerite-Marie was the only one who would comment, and even she did it sotto voce. It seemed to me that the sisters were actually quite protective of Sister Superior, recognizing I think that she was a troubled woman, so they tolerated her outbursts. When she was in one of her agitated moments she became highly critical. Breakfast and supper were eaten in silence, but as the midday meal was shared with the lay teachers who joined us in the refectory, there was general, often quite noisy, conversation.

"What's the matter with you all?" she burst out one evening at supper, interrupting the reader, who put her book down in astonishment. "I've never heard such banal and self-centred conversation as that at midday. You sounded like a group of old spinsters."

"Perhaps that's because we are a group of old spinsters," volunteered one hardy soul.

She ignored the remark. "Half of you were missing at Vespers today and there were several not at Mass this morning."

"We had a staff meeting after school and we took the seniors to Mass at the cathedral. You knew about this, Sister Superior."

"We just need to have a reassessment of our attitude and spirituality I feel there is a real slipping, a general inattention to detail; we haven't had a Chapter of Faults for weeks." She paused. "We'll have one tomorrow."

There was a general groan, which she ignored.

We duly met for the Chapter in the community room. It didn't go according to plan. The young nuns, myself included, went first. Then, on her knees, our charming artist nun began her *culpa*.

"I have been lacking…" She paused. "Lacking… lacking, well struggling…" She paused again.

"With your memory, obviously, my dear." Sister Marguerite-Marie's sly interjection convulsed us all, but the penitent was outraged.

"Well, really! I appeal to you, Sister Superior. How can I go on after that?"

The Chapter resumed, but it certainly didn't have the gravitas that characterized those in the Mother House.

I was asked once by another of my companions if I was scandalized by the difference between St Julien and the Noviciate. Did it bother or trouble me? I had spent a busy morning with students and then helped in the kitchen till teatime. Sister Marguerite-Marie had taken me with her to Benediction at a lovely little Norman church in town and we said our rosary together on the way back. I had even managed my spiritual reading, which sometimes got squeezed out. The community chanted Vespers, as we often did when it was fine, on the flat roof of the convent. So no, it didn't trouble me at all: I found it all wonderful.

"Shouldn't I ask permission?" I said tentatively, when invited to accompany someone on an errand.

"No, it'll be all right. I am sure Sister Superior knows you're with me; someone will tell her. You can tell her yourself at recreation." She saw my uncertainty. "Look, Sister Eleanor, Sister Superior is desperately busy; we are a big community and this is a large school. Imagine if she were constantly interrupted by people asking for permission to do things. She trusts us to be sensible. Tell her at the end of the day. If she disapproves she'll say so, in which case she'll blame me. The Noviciate is different; there you are learning the rules and the Rule. Here, if someone has to go out unexpectedly and may be absent for some time, they find another sister and leave a message." She patted my shoulder reassuringly.

This explanation and behaviour seemed to me eminently practical and I learned was much the same in all our congregation's houses in France, big or little, but I was to discover, to my cost, that this attitude had not travelled well across the Channel.

I was so settled in St Julien, I began to hope that I had been forgotten in England and would stay on indefinitely in France. It was quite unrealistic. I was clearly under-employed in the school, but had no qualifications for anything else. Inevitably, one warm evening in late August, Sister Superior drew me into her study and gently told me that I would be returning to the Mother House the following day. Such moves were always done swiftly in community to avoid protracted farewells and minimize periods of disruption. Reverend Mother General would see me in the afternoon, I was told. Sister Marguerite-Marie helped me to pack. She was bracingly reassuring but stern with my tears.

"You're a nun, for goodness' sake; we take these things in our stride. We go where our Superiors send us. It's been fun having you here and good for you too, but what use are you to us, when all's said and done? You would have had to leave us for training, which is what will happen to you in England." Then she gave me a brisk hug and the inevitable holy picture.

I left St Julien with real regret, but on reflection I realized that it had only been an interlude. I had just been passing through. At the Mother House I discovered to my acute disappointment that Sister Mistress of Novices was on holiday, but Sister Marie-Suzanne greeted me warmly and I spent a lovely evening with Sisters Susan, Clare, Georgette, and Annie. I had to wait until the next day to see Reverend Mother General. She merely told me that I would be returning to England and that Mother Henrietta would give me my "obedience".

It was Sister Marie-Germaine who walked with me to the station; unpredictable as ever, she was friendly and kind.

"I don't want to go back," I said.

"I know, but we are not here to do what we want and you have your place there. Besides, you'll be nearer your family."

Selfishly, I thought this was not necessarily a plus.

CHAPTER 21

Wretchedness in Romiley

I arrived at Manchester airport on a bleak, sunless day and stood disconsolately outside the terminal in the cold. It began to rain. Eventually a taxi driver took pity on me.

"Is somebody picking you up, Sister?"

"I am expecting someone."

"Just say the word and I'll take you wherever you want to go."

I had been assured that Mother Henrietta, the Mother Provincial based at Mary-Mount Convent in Liverpool, would meet me. I had no idea how far Liverpool was from Manchester, so was reluctant to take up the friendly offer from the taxi driver.

The nun who answered the telephone at Mary-Mount when I phoned, after half an hour in the steady rain, sounded put out. "We were expecting you tomorrow! I'll get Mother. We were *told* tomorrow." I began wonder if I was to be left at the airport until the next day.

"Sorry, I'm here today I'm afraid."

Then to my great relief I heard Mother Henrietta's cheerful Lancashire voice.

"Get a taxi, Sister. We are pleased to have you back. What a homecoming, poor child. We'll make it up to you when you get here!"

And they did. It was an affectionate welcome and the depression that had flooded me as I stood waiting at the airport evaporated in the warm friendliness.

My "obedience" was, as I expected, to the convent in Romiley, which I had first visited three years before. I was delighted to be returning. There were faces too that I recognized from elsewhere: some sisters I had known in Filey, and Sister Catriona, who had danced for us in France. Together with other companions from the Noviciate, now professed nuns, we were a young community. It was lovely to be back. Sister Anna greeted me rapturously. The feeling was mutual: she had been instrumental in bringing me into religious life and I owed her a great deal.

During my time in France there had been a change in the community. Sister Anna was no longer Sister Superior. Sister Marie the cook had been appointed her successor. The usual practice was for a new Sister Superior to be imported from another convent and the outgoing Sister Superior to be moved to take up responsibility in her place, so often, once named Superior, a nun tended to remain one, just moving from convent to convent. In human terms, this had pros and cons. A competent woman was valued and recognized, and communities knew they were getting someone with experience who could be relied on to govern sensibly. However, if there wasn't a slot for an outgoing Superior, she stayed put. Some more than others found it difficult to return to the ranks, as it were.

There were certainly more suitable nuns in the community who could have replaced Sister Anna more effectively than poor Sister Marie. But it was felt, at the time, that Sister Anna was essential to the wellbeing of both the school and the community, so she remained. That she was extremely popular was indisputable. She had an easy charm and a bubbling enthusiasm that was difficult to resist. She was considered an asset to the school; but her continued presence in Romiley after her mandate expired was, in many people's opinion, a very big mistake.

Sister Marie was a devout, hardworking, sensible nun who inspired quiet affection and respect, but she was completely unsuited to the new task with which she had been burdened. It was a thoughtless act. This calm, pleasant woman became apprehensive and anxious. It had obviously been recognized that she might not be up to the task, so Sister Anna had been given an unofficial role: that of being responsible for the sisters in temporal vows. In theory this would relieve the new Sister Superior of some of the weight of her duties. In fact she abrogated all responsibility and any demand or request for anything, no matter how insignificant, she referred to Sister Anna, who thus remained de facto Sister Superior. Great effort was made by her to shore up the crumbling authority of the new Superior and she did it with her usual delightful smile and gentle manner. Nevertheless it involved the two of them in whispered conversations apart and generated a feeling of unease that later degenerated into resentment.

For the older members of the community, it wasn't a very great problem. Being well established in their routine, they needed little input from either Sister Superior or Sister Anna, but for the newcomers who needed to test the boundaries, to find a framework within which they could operate, to have all requests met with "I'll ask Sister Anna" or, inversely, "I'll just ask Sister Superior" was disconcerting.

For me, this state of affairs was not immediately a big issue. Initially I was too busy trying to adapt to the "English" way of being a nun. There was no social interaction with the lay staff of the school, three of whom were actually resident within the convent. They ate apart from us. Although I could see that if they were with us for every meal it would have implications for the Great Silence at breakfast, and our intimate community life would be compromised, I did find it odd that they ate in a very large sunny room with gracious stone mullioned bay windows. We, on the other hand, were crammed claustrophobically into a room with no natural light that to my eyes seemed little bigger than a broom cupboard.

At recreation I struggled with the banality of conversation. There seemed to be nothing discussed outside the narrow confines of the community. There was little talk about the school or what had happened during the day, and none at all about the Vatican Council decrees, although all documents had been promulgated and printed and the Catholic press was in a ferment of excitement. There was no discussion of local events in the parish. No opinions were expressed about possible changes to our Constitutions, apart from those relating to the new habits, which we learned were being made at great expense and were no improvement at all on the old ones. We were rigorously discouraged from making any reference to other communities and when one sister was unwise enough to make some completely anodyne remark about her previous Sister Superior, she was frozen out with a terrifying silence. I could see that any reference to St Julien would meet with the same heavy disapproval.

Another major adaptation for me was the loss of French. I felt it slipping away from me like melting snow and I grieved for it like a lost friend. The English translation of the Office Book was actually good, but I longed for the familiar sound of the psalms in French and couldn't warm to it. But it was spiritually that I felt most bereft. The sisters were dedicated, consecrated women – I could see that – but there seemed none of the dynamic open-hearted commitment and the spiritual exchanges that I was so used to. I felt alien and alienated. In the main, in England, we didn't discuss our feelings, and even our views tended to be shyly expressed. But I had become used to the warm, exuberant, sometimes emotional outpourings that were so common in France, and I missed them dreadfully.

There were several sisters in the community whom I could have spoken to, if I had thought about it. Sister Mary-Frances, the headmistress, with her cool reason and advice, could have helped if I had had the sense to approach her, but I found her cold. Sister Florence, who taught art, was great fun and I got on well with her, but she could get strangely hysterical about things.

One afternoon, as I was standing talking to Sister Anna, she arrived breathless and red faced in the hall, dragging two sheepish looking sixth-formers behind her.

"Sister Anna," she shrieked. "I've just found these girls talking through the fence in the field to two *boys*!"

Quite what she thought was so terrible about this I cannot imagine, although I knew there was an unwritten rule that there should be no fraternizing with boys within the grounds. As all the interaction had been through a wire fence, that rule didn't appear to have been broken. The whole thing seemed so ridiculous I began to laugh; even Sister Anna was hard put to keep her face straight.

"I'll deal with it, Sister, thank you." Then she told the girls: "Go back to your classrooms, and don't do it again." I felt she might have added, "At least don't do it where you might get caught!"

At last, desperate for some advice, I asked Sister Superior if I could write to Sister Mistress of Novices in France. She inevitably referred to Sister Anna, who, smiling gently, said, "Oh, I don't think so, Sister. You are here now. You can always talk to me." But that was the problem. I couldn't.

Sometimes the community was involved in arcane activities. Around Christmas time we were armed with baskets full of tinned produce, largesse to dispense to the elderly living in local sheltered accommodation. I thought it was condescending toward the recipients and demeaning to us, but it was a custom, so along with another sister I went. Knocking at one door we heard the occupant shuffling to open it.

"Wait, wait," she cried, panic-stricken that she might miss us. "Don't go away." She was lonely and longing for company and quite indifferent to the tinned peaches. I felt we should be visiting her every day and not just playing Lady Bountiful at Christmas.

Another charming, well-preserved woman, desperate for us to stay longer, offered us a glass of sherry. The nun who was with me refused, but I accepted with alacrity. My companion reported me to Sister Anna and Sister Superior when we got back, both of whom said sternly that my action was inappropriate.

"You know we don't eat or drink in front of seculars and certainly not alcohol!"

"It's never a problem in France," I protested.

"This is England, Sister; this is how we do it here."

I started to find life very difficult in community, and this dissatisfaction troubled me. In the quiet of the chapel or in my own room, I began to feel that I was seriously failing with regard to obedience. Certainly humility seemed to have gone out of the window. I felt deeply troubled.

I had also fallen foul of the French teacher, a lay woman. I was due to sit the GCE in November and attended her classes. We had met briefly before I entered the community. The first morning she greeted me with, "*Vous avez pris pas mal d'embonpoint, chère Soeur*" (You've put on quite some weight, my dear Sister). I thought it insultingly rude, even if it was true. She was a good teacher but she took badly to my questioning some aspect of colloquial usage. I thought her a vain and stupid woman, and she thought me a cocky and arrogant nun. Probably both those opinions were justified.

The malaise in the community became more evident, and little by little the community began to polarize: young professed on one side and older nuns on the other. One of the sisters, who seemed to live virtually in Sister Anna's pocket, relayed back all the discontent, pretty well word for word. By this time I was barely able to conceal my disenchantment. Then, one night shortly after Christmas, at about ten o'clock when I was already in bed, Sister Superior knocked on my door.

Nervously and with what seemed a mixture of relief and embarrassment, she announced, "Tomorrow, after breakfast, Mother Henrietta is coming to collect you. You are going to Liverpool, to Mary-Mount. You can pack in the morning. Goodnight."

I lay for an hour in some trepidation. Was I going to be sent packing? Could I be sent away mid-vows? Had I caused scandal? I did, though, feel some relief. The short time I had been in Romiley I considered to have been wretched. Mary-Mount could only be better.

I felt quite cheerful in the morning. I had no idea if the community knew of my imminent departure, but I thought not, as nobody said goodbye, to my relief.

And so, after barely three months, I left Romiley and never went back.

CHAPTER 22

A Happy House and a Change of Direction

The Liverpool convent Mary-Mount was the base for Mother Henrietta, the Provincial Superior. She, along with two councillors, governed the English Province. The convent had been opened as a hostel for working girls and professional women who needed somewhere safe to live, on the style of a YWCA. It also took in a few elderly lady boarders.

It was a large, handsome nineteenth-century building, in leafy Mossley Hill. I always felt there was something comfortable and comforting about Mary-Mount. It had the slightly rundown air of an elegant woman fallen on hard times. In the sixties, the city had not begun its regeneration and was rapidly crumbling, if not into the sea (although that was certainly true around the silent, empty, desolate docks) then certainly into the ground. Vast swathes of the city were being demolished; whole streets of little Victorian back-to-backs torn down and communities relocated or, as they saw it, destroyed. Families who had lived in a particular district for generations were being rehoused in hideous and soul-destroying Stalinesque tower blocks, while elegant Georgian houses, previously home to the wealthy merchants who had made their money from sugar and slaves, clung to their past glory, despite peeling stucco and multiple occupancy. Mary-Mount with its determined but shabby gentility seemed all of a piece with it.

The convent comprised a community of a dozen or so sisters of all ages and stages of religious profession, including those who were undergoing teaching or nursing training in the city. The physical burden of running the hostel fell in the main to the younger nuns, as the older sisters were almost too frail for any strenuous work. The exception was Sister Bernadette, known affectionately as Bernie.

Delightful, small, and permanently cheerful, she bustled about, hardworking and diligent despite her years. Her sunny nature, even when she grumbled, was irrepressible. Intelligent and quick-witted, she was generous in her pride and admiration for the qualifications achieved by the student nuns and felt no envy for the educational opportunities of which she had been deprived. She had left school at thirteen and when she entered religious life, the congregation was still divided into choir and lay sisters, the latter being responsible for the manual work in the community. This was a hangover from the days when gentlewomen entering a convent took their maids in with them! Bernie had been a lay sister. She told me once that everybody seemed to think it a great privilege to have been upgraded to a choir nun but, as she pointed out, "You can honour Our Lord just as well scrubbing floors as singing the Office; probably better when I hear some of them singing in chapel!"

The only time I heard her a little sour in her comments was when, with sweat staining her bandeau and running down her cheeks, her arms up to the elbow in soap suds (there was no dishwasher in Mary-Mount then), she said, "If there was a degree in washing-up, they'd all be out here helping. Maybe they'll give me one!"

I grew to be very fond of her. She had a wonderful head of thick brown hair, peppered with grey, which I helped her to wash. We shared a bedroom for a time, and I would watch her plait it so it hung like a thick rope, very nearly to the small of her back. Deep down, she was very proud of it, a small and charming vanity.

Among the other members of the community were the nuns training as nurses or teachers. There was also a small group who had made their final vows but had not yet reached the stage of "elders". They didn't benefit from any of the advantages of the young professed, who were regularly sent on training courses and to attend religious conferences. Sister Margaret was one such. Plump and listless, she was nevertheless a sensitive woman who wrote undistinguished poetry and made pious, pretty Christmas cards, but who seemed, sadly, to have done nothing with her life. I don't know if she had ever been a teacher but she certainly hadn't been a nurse. She suffered from a permanent undefined vague ill health that sometimes necessitated several days in bed, probably some digestive complaint, which nobody took very seriously.

"I'm going to ask for a strong white bottle," she would say when the doctor who made regular visits was expected. We teased her about asking him to put plenty of gin in it and the "strong white bottle", probably a form of Milk of Magnesia, became a euphemism for any remedy. She took our teasing in very good part. I think she was probably undervalued in the community and suffered for it.

Another young nun, a mainstay of the house, was one of the most energetic young women I'd ever met, always busy and yet always ready to help. We once stuck a label on her back that someone had picked up at an ESSO petrol station. It read "I've got a tiger in my tank" and it stayed on all day. She was furious when she discovered it, as it had been appreciated not only by the community but also the residents.

The convent was dominated by the overwhelming personality of Mother Henrietta. She should have been detached from the day-to-day running of the house, which was the Sister Superior's job, as she was the Provincial Superior in charge of the overall organization of the congregation in England, Ireland, and Wales. It was not that she was interfering; it was more that her temperament was so active, she just didn't know how to take a back seat. Such was her presence that it seemed natural to refer to her for everything.

Mother Henrietta was an extraordinary woman. Short and stout with a ruddy complexion and keen pale blue eyes, she was the object of respect, admiration, and affection not just in her community but among all those who came into contact with her throughout the city. That over-used word "charisma" was not too strong for her. She had the ability to make people like her, even love her, despite her faults and failings. She could be amazingly obstinate and was often hasty in her decisions. She had complete confidence in her own (sometimes faulty) judgment, but she was warm, sympathetic, loving, encouraging, and above all deeply devout. On a practical level, the wellbeing of the nuns under her jurisdiction was very important to her, and she prided herself, with some justification, on making herself available to all of them and sending as many as possible to acquire some form of qualification, even if it were only a night-class diploma.

The first years of her religious life had been spent in France teaching English. During the war she was one of only a handful of British nuns not interned. She managed this by a mixture of bluff and luck. As she had dual English/Irish nationality, she persuaded the German authority of her Irishness, and when they finally began to question it, reverted to, "I'm a nun – what possible threat could I be? Besides, I'm needed in the school. I'll come in to the area GHQ to report every month." They began to insist on every week. "Not possible," this amazing woman replied. "I'm so busy this time of year. I'm sure you understand, exams, you know. No, once a month will be fine, really."

Bemused, they went away and she was left in peace. She returned to England after the war and became Sister Superior at Mary-Mount, remaining so for ten years. Then she was named Mother Provincial in the same convent, so it was unsurprising that she should consider Mary-Mount her own undisputed patch.

It was she whom I faced the morning after my ignominious departure from Romiley. Mother Henrietta saw me in her comfortable study. She sat me down, then, folding her plump hands over her plumper bosom, she stared steadily at me.

"I've been rethinking," she said. "I really don't think teaching is for you. It's a jungle out there in those schools. No…" She paused. Then, pointing her index finger at me, she announced triumphantly, "Nursing, that's the thing for you!"

I stared at her in horror. "Mother, you can't have thought this through. I couldn't cope with all that blood splashing about, nose bleeds and operations and so on." I was beginning to babble. "I can tell you, it was only because I couldn't see what was dripping into the bottle that I managed to donate blood when I was a novice, and I felt sick as a parrot when it was going on. The only reason I didn't pass out was because I was already lying down!"

She halted my breathless frantic delivery with a raised hand. "No, no," she said soothingly, "it's nothing like that these days. It's all bloodless surgery. Richard Dimbleby did a programme about it on *Panorama*. Everything is sealed off with diathermy needles! Why don't you give it a go? If you are not happy, I promise I'll take you out, and we'll think of something else."

The voice of authority for many nuns in those days was, in descending order: the Pope, the Superior General of their own congregation, and Richard Dimbleby, whose unctuous reassuring tones inspired total confidence. She was 100 per cent wrong about the bloodlessness of hospitals in general, and operating theatres in particular, but she sold it to me.

"I've great hope for you, Sister Eleanor," she said. "I knew you'd see it God's way! You've got an interview at Broadgreen tomorrow and will be able to start in February."

She had a way of putting her hand up to her ear and pressing it, like sports commentators on television receiving incoming information. It always made me feel she had a sort of hotline to the Almighty, which she might well have had for all I know.

So I joined two others from the community: Sister Catherine and Sister Anne-Marie, who were already training at the hospital.

Sister Mary, Mother Henrietta's secretary, was delighted. "It'll be great," she said, "having you here. We'll have such fun." I hadn't heard anyone talk about fun since I'd left St Julien. Certainly

Mary-Mount had a French feel about it. Mother Henrietta's years in France, combined with her own robust view of life, had rubbed off on the community, who, all in all, seemed a cheerful and relaxed group. Sister Teresa, the cook, was young, fat, and jolly, with a beautiful pink and white complexion and the lovely Irish combination of blue eyes and dark lashes. I don't think she enjoyed being a cook, and on a day-to-day basis was not very good at it, although she could produce wonderful stuff when called upon. She was wasted in the kitchen. "Well, isn't that grand," she greeted my news with a tranquil lack of surprise. "If Mother thinks it's for you, I'm sure you'll do just fine."

Within days I was kitted out with half a dozen white cotton dresses, white veils, and aprons. Then finally, with some degree of trepidation, I began my nursing training.

Mother Henrietta was right. I loved it from the very beginning.

CHAPTER 23

Broadgreen, Val Doonican, and Other Oddities

Broadgreen had started life as a fever hospital and even in the sixties parts of it were old fashioned, still retaining the twenty-eight-bedded "Nightingale" wards. They were austere, almost stark; certainly they afforded patients little privacy. But this design, now obsolete, had many advantages. A nurse looking up the ward could see immediately the status of each of her patients and they in turn could see her. She knew who was eating or not eating, who needed help or who was in discomfort. If she didn't notice, there was always some alert patient to bellow, "Hey, Nurse, Mr J's gone blue again!" or "Miss M's dropped all her pills and they're rolling about under her bed!"

Postoperative care in those days meant patients often spent several days in bed, so their comfort was paramount. Any nurse who neglected to straighten a wrinkled sheet, plump up a pillow, or lift a patient into a more comfortable position would be considered in dereliction of duty, particularly as you could see at a glance who had slipped down the bed and was in danger of being suffocated by their own bedding.

Nursing auxiliaries were almost unknown. Student nurses did everything, bar scrubbing floors: damp dusting; bed making; bedpan rounds; "back" rounds, which meant treatment of pressure areas: buttocks, heels, elbows, and shoulder blades. We must have got through gallons of surgical spirit in a year and more talcum than the whole of the eighteenth century used for powdering wigs. We washed and bathed patients and put them on and off bedpans. These were heavy metal objects that the monstrous machine in the sluice was alleged to clean, but which failed so often and so spectacularly that we were usually obliged to scour them out ourselves. Our hands became raw from the disinfectant we used, a vicious fluid called Lysol, quite excoriating even diluted. I later discovered that it was often the measure of choice taken by desperate girls in a vain effort to rid their vaginas of sperm after an incautious coupling or, occasionally undiluted, to procure a miscarriage. The burns were dreadful and it didn't work.

Practically, the regularity of the shape of the ward made cleaning and nursing easier. There was no need for a "nursing station" because we were a permanent presence "on the floor", all within sight and sound of each other. The Ward Sister directed operations like a regimental Sergeant Major. As each nurse came on duty and reported in, she was given her orders. As every task was completed, she returned to the Ward Sister, the staff nurse, or in some instances the senior nurse to ask for further instructions. The cleaners, responsible for the floors, were formidable women and often more feared than the sternest Ward Sister. It was a brave nurse who walked boldly up the passage on a newly washed floor without making some craven apology. The first cleaner I encountered, who put the fear of God into me, was short and burly with an enormous port wine birthmark across her cheek.

"You needn't think you can walk over my floor, Sister, without as much as a 'sorry' just because you're a nun," she snarled.

There were several nuns from different congregations who began their training with me, among them two sweet, shy, and gentle Ugandans. There were in all about twenty-five first-year students. We nuns, in white ankle-length dresses, our heads veiled, seemed a world apart from the mini-skirted youngsters, their white caps pinned jauntily onto their improbable "bee-hive" hair. This was drawn well back from their forehead – the rule was "no hair on the collar or loose round the face". They had scrubbed cheeks and no jewellery, except a wedding ring if married (none were). They wore green dresses with stiff white collars and starched aprons, their tiny waists cinched with a green webbing belt; legs, various in shape, were all encased in thick black tights and ended in severe, crêpe-soled, black lace-up shoes. There wasn't a fat one among them and they all looked, from the rear anyway, unbelievably like Barbara Windsor in *Carry On Doctor*.

Initially we had some weeks of preliminary training in the School of Nursing before being let loose on a ward. Every year we had four weeks of study in the school, but apart from that our training was "in-service". We were monitored by periodic visits from the Sister Tutors, plus a written report, which we never saw, from each of the wards that we worked on.

The nursing day worked around a three-shift system: an early, a late, and the loathed "split" shift, which meant you worked till lunchtime then came back on at 4:30 p.m. and worked through till the night staff came on at 7:15 p.m. The night shift was a twelve-hour spell. We had a day and a half off every week and I have no idea what I earned, because everything was paid into the convent account and I gave my payslip unopened to Sister Superior.

When I was on an "early", I left Mary-Mount before 7:00 a.m. in order to be changed and on duty at 7:30. Sometimes I was on my own; on other occasions Sister Catherine and Sister Anne-Marie were with me. On Sundays we caught the bus at Penny Lane and, yes, there was a fire station there! The street sign was pinched so often that in the end the council stopped replacing it.

We had to fit our prayers in as best we could. We rose with the community as usual at 5:30 a.m., so had time for Laudes and meditation before leaving home. I said my rosary going down the road, but my examination of conscience and spiritual reading were often neglected, although I tried to make up for it on my days off. What I missed most frequently, although my intentions were good, was daily Mass. If I had a late shift, it was no problem – I had community Mass in chapel; but with an early shift it was difficult to find an evening Mass and on a split shift it was even harder.

There was an afternoon Mass at a local church at 3:00 p.m., which gave me just about enough time to scamper back to be on duty for 4:30, but I usually fell asleep in the nurses' sitting room once I'd had lunch, and woke just in time to have a cup of tea before going back on duty. I know that other nursing nuns were diligent about their attendance and I felt guilty about my lapses, but although I sometimes managed it, more often than not I was obliged to tell kind, gentle Sister Superior that I had missed Mass. She was surprisingly tolerant about it, having herself, for reasons beyond her control during internment in Besançon during the war, been deprived of Holy Communion, but I knew it to be a failure on my part, particularly as I had the example of others who never missed Mass at all.

"Well?" Sister Mary was waiting for me after my first day on the wards. "What have you got?"

"Male orthopaedic."

"Dear God! All those bedridden men with weights attached to their legs and Heath Robinson frames suspending their limbs, not to mention bolts through their arms and legs…"

"Yes! How do you know?"

"I've seen it all on *Panorama*; how do you think?" She laughed aloud at my face.

Although I didn't tell her, the smell of male sweat, heavy morning breath, and occasionally the delicate and not unpleasant odour of semen made us all catch our breath till we could get the windows open, make the beds, and change the sheets.

"My God!" Night Sister used to say at her 2:00 a.m. round, eyeing the rumpled beds and listening to the snoring. "Why should Britain tremble?" Obviously a rhetorical question!

Most of the men on male orthopaedic were young. Many were victims of car or industrial accidents, and a few older ones had broken hips, repaired in those days with a "pin and plate". Hip replacements were unknown. They were immobilized for weeks. Some patients were on traction because of back pain, due perhaps to a collapsed or slipped disc. This seemed to me a modern form of being on the rack and it never seemed to do much good, although it looked dramatic. Modern thinking considers it the worst thing to do for such conditions and all effort is made to keep a patient mobile.

I came home one day with interesting news: "Mother, would you believe it! We look after injured players on the Liverpool and Everton football teams, Mr Heron for one and Mr Arnold for the other. I can't remember which for which!"

Mother Henrietta was an obsessional fan. She did the pools regularly, shades of Sister Yvonne in the Noviciate; not for herself, she assured me, but for the wellbeing of all. She never missed matches if Liverpool or Everton were televised. Indeed the entire community were riveted to the screen and, thanks to her, we soon became both knowledgable and addicted. In 1966 the World Cup was not just the focus of recreation but the only conversation at mealtimes, when we had "permission to speak". Some of us even grasped the rules of "offside".

Usually we only watched the television programmes Mother approved. Her attachment to *Panorama* was more to do with her unshakable belief in Richard Dimbleby than with any real interest in current affairs. We watched Val Doonican because he was Irish and she liked his voice, although was not so sure about his dreadful knitted jumpers. She had a soft spot for *Dr Finlay's Casebook* and, daringly, for Dave Allen, whom she thought at heart was a devout Catholic because he always finished his programme with: "May your gods go with you."

Among the young sisters in the house I became close to several who, like me, enjoyed the television, when we could express our preferences, which we were occasionally allowed to do. Sister Lucinda enjoyed anything with some spirit in it, and gentle, sunny-natured Sister Caroline once confided in me that although she loved *Dr Finlay's Casebook*, the bend at the end of Bill Simpson's nose bothered her. I never saw it again without sniggering. Sister Irene was interestingly objective about *Panorama*. I don't think she was as convinced as Mother Henrietta about the infallibility of Richard Dimbleby. These were all nuns who had done their noviciate in Ireland; it was my loss that I never got to know them better.

I pressed determinedly for some drama, and insistently, with some back-up from others, for *Cathy Come Home*. With some reluctance Mother Henrietta agreed. We went to bed as usual in silence and had no opportunity to discuss it for a couple of days, by which time the impact had faded. We did manage to watch an amazingly funny play, on the strength of it having John Gielgud in it, which meant therefore it was "classical". It was called *The Mayfly and the Frog* and had a pretty round-faced young actress called Felicity Kendal in it, who, Mother Henrietta said, "had promise".

After a long day at the hospital, it was comforting to return to the cheerful, busy atmosphere of Mary-Mount, where I melted into convent life as if my absence was incidental, but it seemed a universe away from what I faced on the ward. Curiously, although everyone enjoyed anecdotal accounts of amusing incidents, serious issues of life and death, pain, sorrow, and loss were glossed over by many in the community, so my two lives seemed completely separate. It was as if the human dramas would somehow trouble the calm order of community existence. Occasionally, one or other of the sisters would ask some perceptive question and I would try to answer honestly, but it was difficult for them to grasp the sense of it all. They were hearing tales as unreal as fiction and as unrelated to their lives as a story.

The community was a warm place with real charm and a robust spirituality, but even with Mother Henrietta at the helm, there were things that jarred and to some extent she was the cause. Only she and Sister Mary, her secretary, could drive. She saw no need for anyone else to do so and indeed, apart from the sisters going to the hospital or to college, the other nuns rarely left the house. If Sister Mary needed to go out, she would come into the community room and commandeer someone to accompany her, as it was considered inappropriate for a nun to drive on her own. If Mother went out, it was invariably Sister Mary who went with her. The car, a large black Ford Zephyr saloon, had been bought for the community by a pleasant wealthy widow who was actually Mother's own sister. In fact she bought a new car for the community every couple of years, but, given the circumstances, it wasn't surprising that the car seemed more like a personal gift, and it would have been unnatural for Mother Henrietta not to feel subconsciously that that was the case. Certainly the car was used to transport sisters around, but it would have been unthinkable to ask for it or to ask to learn to drive it. There was an Irish odd-job man who drove it if neither Mother nor Sister Mary was free. He cleaned it regularly and always referred to it as "Mother's car".

There was also a dog: a fat, spoiled, bad-tempered Labrador called Bijou. Pets were expressly forbidden by the Rule, although I knew that many of our houses had them. Mother justified the animal on the grounds that the convent, being full of women, both nuns and laity, might need protection from intruders. However, Bijou, overweight and lazy, would have been useless as a guard dog, particularly as he lived in her study and only left it when she or Sister Mary came into the main house. He had been an enchanting puppy, but grew enormous and untrustworthy from lack of exercise. He was overfed and was, to all intents and purposes, Mother's dog. I, who had grown up in a home where there were always animals, both detested and feared him. He would lumber about, barking at both residents and nuns. Although most of them seemed sanguine about his behaviour, he had snapped at me on several occasions, and I avoided him. I dived into the lavatory if I saw or heard him coming.

Unlike that of some of the other sisters, Mother's health seemed good; she was certainly indulged at table. On the other hand, I thought *our* diet was seriously lacking. Apart from Sundays, when we had the traditional roast dinner, our food, although plentiful, was limited in variety. There were lots of carbohydrates but very little in the way of fresh fruit and vegetables. Some of the older, frailer sisters could well have benefited from the first-class protein that ended up on Mother's plate. She usually had a completely different meal from the rest of the community and was quite shameless about eating steak and grilled tomatoes while we dined on bread, butter, and fried onions or mashed potato. Occasionally she and Sister Mary brought back fish and chips for us all, because Mother liked them. By the time they got home, our supper was congealing and soggy.

Several sisters clearly suffered from eating disorders. Sister Mary, as lean as a greyhound, would wave away a proffered dish with the back of her hand and an expression of distaste. Sister Isabelle, young, tall, and beautiful, dropped her weight steadily as she ate less and less, emulating Sister Mary, whom I think she regarded a role model. Nobody seemed aware of this aberrant behaviour, until one day it was forced to our attention.

One quiet but pleasant sister was desperately thin and had the pasty complexion and poor skin of the seriously undernourished. She seemed to eat nothing but bread and butter, and very little of that. Eventually she became ill and was hospitalized. I visited her with two or three other sisters and, seeing her in her nightdress, was aware of how shockingly emaciated she was. The medical staff expressed serious concerns about her state of health, both physical and mental. About a fortnight after her hospitalization, it was announced that she would not be returning either to Mary-Mount or to any other community. The doctors, Mother Henrietta said, felt that the religious life was detrimental to her health and accordingly she would be relieved of her vows and returned to her family.

This news was received in stunned silence. The Rule stated quite categorically that once a nun was admitted to final vows, she had the right to remain in the congregation in sickness or in health until her death. The only reason she could be dismissed was for grave scandal, and the Rule emphasized "grave".

"Here's a thing," said Sister Margaret. "She's been eating like a sparrow for years. Anyone could see she wasn't eating, but nothing was said. She did her work and was a good nun as far as anyone could tell. Then she goes into hospital for treatment and some doctor, who knows nothing about her and even less about the religious life, decides that it's doing her harm and she's sent away! I think I'll keep quiet about my stomach from now on!"

Sister Bernie was equally outspoken: "Poor girl! She was ill. God help us if we are all to be sent away because we get sick."

We were a sombre lot at recreation that night. I managed to get a few words with Sister Elizabeth, two or three years my senior in religion, with whom I got on well. She was at teacher-training college and I knew she'd give me a sensible opinion.

"What's all this about?" I asked her. "How can it happen? How can a decision be made like that, so swiftly? Did it go to the Mother House?"

"Oh yes, I'm sure it did. Mother would have phoned and spoken to Reverend Mother General."

"Well then?"

"Then they'd have taken Mother's advice and asked her opinion."

"What about that poor sister? Didn't she have any right of appeal? She had taken final vows, for heaven's sake."

"Maybe she didn't want to appeal. We don't know – maybe she *was* unhappy, even glad to go. Look what was facing her if she came back. Imagine being forced to eat; imagine Sister Mary standing over you while you struggled to get food down. Look at it from Mother's point of view. Suppose she ignored the doctors and brought the poor sister home and she died. People do die from anorexia. Mother would carry the responsibility; she would take the blame."

Sister Elizabeth's calm assessment soothed me, but once again I saw with apprehension the disappearance, shrouded in secrecy, of someone who seemed vulnerable and in need of our loving support, not our censure. Within a week she seemed forgotten. I never heard her name mentioned again. It was as if she had never been among us.

CHAPTER 24

Renewal of Vows and "Night Duty"

A few months after beginning my nursing training, I renewed my vows. It was a year since I had made my first profession and after the disaster in Romiley, when I had seriously doubted that I had any future in the congregation. I was overjoyed to be committing myself once again to God and the religious life. Our vows were received during High Mass by a beaming Mother Henrietta, delegating for Reverend Mother General. It was a very happy day in the community, which we celebrated with one of the cook's good meals, songs, and laughter, and quite large quantities of Babycham, which Mother Henrietta believed, for some reason known only to herself, was non-alcoholic.

At the hospital I relaxed into a happy and busy existence. We changed wards about every six weeks in order that our training should encompass every aspect of nursing care. It was always unnerving changing wards. There was a new Sister to get to know and new techniques to master. Sister Meaham, female medical Ward Sister, was formidable but a devoted and hardworking nurse. She used to say she hated it when we were not busy. "It's when my ladies are likely to be neglected. Everybody relaxes. I don't want relaxed nurses; I want diligent, observant, caring nurses. Above all, nurses who look for work to do rather than being pleased to have an easy day."

She looked challengingly at me. All I could say was, "Right, Sister." I never saw her with her sleeves down or her stiff wrist cuffs on, although this was standard for the consultants' round and for Matron's weekly visit. She was proud to say that she was a working Ward Sister. "Not one who sits in the office all day flirting with the registrars." I learned a great deal from her.

Specialization, as we understand it today, was not a big feature of hospital care. Broadgreen was one of several general hospitals in the area. Although some hospitals specialized in certain aspects of medical care, in the main every medical ward would be filled with a variety of cases, treating any condition affecting any part of the body. With a few notable exceptions the same was true of surgical wards; all surgery was treated as one. However, some of the notable exceptions made odd bedfellows! Orthopaedics was on its own, but gynaecology and eye surgery were, bizarrely, housed in the same ward. So a patient having undergone a hysterectomy might find herself in the next bed to a woman having had cataracts removed.

We were very proud of our new state-of-the-art intensive care unit. Broadgreen's specialism was in cardiac and lung surgery. As the regional centre, patients came to us from as far afield as North Wales and the Isle of Man. The twelve-bedded unit was specifically designed for cardiac procedures, although it did take patients undergoing other extensive and complicated surgery. Replacement of diseased heart valves meant open heart surgery, which was still a pioneering procedure in the sixties. We only did about three of such operations a week, first because they took so long, and secondly because the cleaning of the theatre afterwards was such an intensive business.

In the main, only patients with a good chance of survival were operated on, not necessarily those with the sickest hearts. The operation itself was lengthy and patients were nursed for at least twenty-four (often forty-eight) hours on a ventilator until their own breathing was re-established. The unit looked like a scene from *2001: A Space Odyssey,* with bodies hooked up to steel and glass machines, bellows pumping rhythmically, intravenous infusions above and drainage tubes below, the whole place a cacophony of clunking and clicking, oozing and dripping. At night when the unit was quieter, if you stood at a patient's bedside, you could hear the new valve opening and snapping shut again. They were, after all, merely plastic, and although the noise was unnerving, it did at least allow you to know that the apparently moribund patient was indeed alive.

The unit was sometimes as unnerving for the patients as it was for the student nurses. One of the Ugandan nursing nuns, Sister Emmanuel Obote, told me that looking up from dealing with one patient, she saw another one walking away. His pale buttocks were on view as his gown swung open, and he had a large drainage bottle tucked under each arm as he made his way unsteadily toward the end of the ward and freedom. "Mr Babcock," she called. "Stop. Wherever are you going?"

"I'm going home," he said. "The bus stop's just around the corner. I can't stay here. There's a corpse in the next bed, or something that looks like one, and people all attached to machines."

By this time the nun had reached him and managed to grab the drainage bottles to keep them below his chest level, to prevent the fluid running back into whatever cavity it was draining from. Having stated his position, he then slid slowly to the floor, pulling the poor little nun down with him, and passed out.

Two days later he had no memory of this and was fulsome in his praise for what he called the miracle of modern science, which had saved him. "We needn't have worried. They wouldn't have let him on the bus," the Ward Sister announced cheerfully. I felt that there were usually enough of the "halt and the lame" getting on outside the hospital that he'd have stood a particularly good chance of not being noticed at all.

Death, sadly, was common enough that it barely rated a comment over lunch, but an open heart operation was such a big event that the entire hospital knew about it. News of a death, particularly "on the table", was around the place in a flash. One young woman, who was believed to have an excellent chance of surviving the operation, died because when her breastbone was divided by the circular saw, her damaged heart was discovered to have adhered to the underside. The saw sliced straight through and cut it in half. Today, a scan would have revealed the situation

Every few months we had a month of night duty. The shift was 7:30 p.m. until 7:30 a.m. the following morning; we worked eight nights on, then six off; it was a killer. Our time clock had just got adjusted to the new system when it all changed again.

Night duty was the busiest shift because there were so few of us and it was the one that landed us with most responsibility. Apart from the Night Sisters, there were few qualified staff on duty. Usually a third-year student was in charge of a ward, but it was not uncommon for a second-year to be landed with the job and, on more than one occasion, even in my first year I found myself with that heavy responsibility. If we were lucky there were two of us to a ward, but often we were three nurses between two adjacent wards, the junior nurse being a "runner". Her job was to be there when a task needed four hands rather than two. She scampered like a terrier between the two. It was a thankless task, as she was always being berated by one nurse for favouring the other one!

At night, calm descended. There was an intimacy and a more relaxed atmosphere than on any of the day shifts, despite the amount of work. There were no doctors' rounds, tests, or X-rays being done; no visits from Matron or Sister Tutor; no cleaners, and unless patients were on an "urgent note", meaning they were seriously ill and their family had unrestricted access, no visitors. The low lights lent cosiness, even on the surgical wards, when on "theatre days" there might be as many as eight postoperative cases to be nursed. There was still plenty to do, but despite the ubiquitous bedpan round, it all seemed friendlier. Sometimes, daringly, nurses were called by their Christian name, which was unheard of in the daytime. We nuns were supposed to be called "Nurse" followed by our surname, but this dictat from Matron was almost universally ignored. We were called "Sister" or, more usually for both nun and nurse alike, "Love" or occasionally "Petal". Nobody confused us with the Ward Sister. It was only too clear who was number one and, even in her absence, her authority was supreme.

Night Sister did her first round at about 10:00 p.m. in time to check any medication that fell under the category of Dangerous Drugs. She would only reappear at about 2:00 a.m. and 6:00 a.m., unless called for. Some things had to be verified by a qualified nurse, such as blood for a patient having a transfusion. This was kept, rather ghoulishly, in the kitchen fridge, and had to be double-checked. The consequences of giving the wrong blood group were potentially fatal. When the lights were switched off, we set up a little cocoon for ourselves in the centre of the ward, pulling two screens around armchairs and drawing down the green shaded light that gave us just enough illumination to read by. We were surrounded by a concert of steady nocturnal breathing, snoring, and moaning.

It was on night duty that we got to know the patients. When sleep was evasive or if pain, fear, or discomfort kept them awake, they were pleased to talk and all sorts of things spilled out. Make a cup of tea and stand by a bedside, patting a hand reassuringly or smoothing a sheet, and the most intimate details could pour out into the ears of girls of nineteen or twenty whose own life experiences were still so limited. They became the inevitable and sometimes alarmed recipients of expressions of the most private emotions; heard wonderful, sad, or harrowing stories whispered in the intimacy of the dark.

Before we became second-years, we had seen death in all its guises, sometimes gruesomely, sudden devastating haemorrhage or unexpected debilitating collapse. We had performed external cardiac massage, mouth-to-mouth resuscitation, and laid out the dead. I had my mouth clamped to more men in my three years at Broadgreen than I have ever had, before or since. There was no orifice of the human body that we were not intimate with.

Occasionally, nights could be very busy indeed. Hospitals in the area took it in turn to admit emergency cases, both surgical and medical. This was called "being on take". Quite often the Royal Infirmary, when it was their turn, pleaded they were full and the overflow came to us. We were disparaging about this, believing, probably incorrectly, that they only wanted "interesting patients", because they were a teaching hospital with a medical school. Patients were admitted through Casualty (now called A&E) to the wards. There was never any question in Broadgreen of there not being enough room. The porters brought in extra beds and they were placed down the centre of the ward. It was not uncommon to have three or more supplementary patients by morning. They had to be admitted, processed, and treated. Patients sometimes came straight from the operating theatre, having undergone surgery. They all needed postoperative care and as we were usually, at the most, two nurses per ward, it was demanding. If a patient was seriously ill and needed individual care, an extra nurse would be sent. Sometimes she was more trouble than she was worth. If she didn't know the ward, everything had to be explained to her and although most of the wards were very similar, at night even small variations were confusing.

Patients who had been unconscious had to be roused every half hour for their vital signs to be recorded. This involved, apart from taking their pulse and blood pressure, shining a light into their eyes to check pupil reaction. Not surprisingly this was often met with vehement protest, particularly if the unconsciousness had been due to an enthusiastic night in the pub or was the consequence of a brawl afterwards. All individuals found unconscious on the street had to be brought in to assess the cause. They were just beginning to get to sleep in a clean dry bed when every thirty minutes or so a torch was flashed in their face and they were asked to open their eyes, count fingers, and squeeze a hand. One man told me roundly to "F*** off", and then, dimly making out my bandeau and veil, gasped, "Oh Mother of Mercy, haven't I sworn at a nun, God forgive me!"

It was said there were more Catholics in Liverpool than in Dublin, and I sometimes thought there were more Irish too. As they had maintained their reputation for boisterous and rowdy behaviour and an ever-ready determination to resolve any disagreement with their bare knuckles, we got a lot of them passing through Casualty.

We weren't supposed to disturb the patients before 6:45 a.m., a rule that was as unrealistic as it was arbitrary. On surgical wards six or seven patients might have to be prepared for theatre. This was particularly time-consuming if there were people going for bowel surgery. The gut had to be as clean as possible, so these patients had to undergo "colonic washout", which could take as long as fifteen to twenty minutes. Strangely, this procedure has become both fashionable and popular today among a certain sector of society, under the more elegant if euphemistic name of "colonic hydrotherapy". Why anyone should enjoy having quite large amounts of water run up into their bowel remains a mystery to me, even if done in the calm and elegant surroundings of a discreet private clinic with pastel-coloured walls and soothing music. Apparently it is considered part of the detox fad popular among the chattering classes.

Apart from this, the ubiquitous bedpan, back, and medicine rounds still had to be done, together with the recordings of blood pressure, pulse, and temperature. Bedridden patients needed to be washed, the ambulant escorted to the bathroom, breakfast served and cleared, the beds straightened and everybody sitting up, hair and teeth brushed, with shining morning faces, ready to greet the Ward Sister when she arrived.

Above all, and most importantly, the senior nurse had to write the report. This was a record of every patient, detailing treatment, medication, and their general condition, including how they had passed the night. It took at least forty minutes. It was clearly impossible to do all this between 6:45 and 7:30 a.m., so we cheated. From 5:30 a.m. onwards, earlier if Night Sister had done her round, we began to tiptoe around, waking the less ill patients first with apologetic grimaces.

"I'm so sorry to disturb you, but I'm going to give you a little wash... take your blood pressure... temperature... pulse!"

The patients were complicit and would call out cheerfully "Let us know when you want us to start the tea, Sister." Traditionally ambulant patients took around the hot drinks trolley both in the morning and in the evening. All of them were amazingly tolerant about being disturbed at this uncivilized hour. As there was no real shortage of nurses or beds, the composition of patients in any ward would include several who weren't particularly ill at all. Patients having undergone routine surgery stayed in hospital for anything up to three weeks, depending on the operation. Nowadays, providing there are no complications, they are dispatched home to be looked after by their relatives or the district nurse sometimes as little as forty-eight hours after major surgery and often with drainage tubes still in situ. Patients on medical wards could be desperately ill, but some were also admitted for tests or for observation or to have a medical condition stabilized, so it was unsurprising that generally the atmosphere was much more upbeat than would be the case today.

Night duty gave me more regular time in Mary-Mount. With several days off, I slid back easily into convent routine. Coming home in the morning to Sister Teresa's warm kitchen, leaning against the stove while she made me a cup of tea, waiting for my hot water bottle, was one of life's great pleasures. Sometimes I found "down and outs" at the back door. Sister Teresa made them huge mugs of sweet tea and enormous fried egg sandwiches. If the weather was bad, they sat just inside. I suggested once to Mother Henrietta that they should be invited in to join the community for breakfast. This idea was received first with hilarity and then, when I persisted, with irritation.

"Good heavens, Sister, we are running a hostel for women, not a shelter for dossers."

"Mother, we could be entertaining angels unawares," I insisted, quoting St Paul.

"I don't think so, Sister. I think it's enough that we feed them and let them get warm. It's all they want."

"All the angels round here go to the Little Sisters of the Poor," added Sister Mary ironically, for good measure.

They were probably right, but it didn't seem very evangelical to me. Although I wouldn't have invited any of the itinerants who frequented Mary-Mount into my own home, this was a convent full of nuns supposedly following the evangelical counsels: *Go and sell everything you own and give the money to the poor... then come, follow me... in so far as you did this to one of the least of these brothers of mine, you did it to me*. I thought they were a little short on taking the good Lord at his word.

CHAPTER 25

A New Broom and Family Worries

As student nuns, we were not allowed to share in the work of the house. Our days off were periods of study and of rest. So we spent hours in a bright little "parlour" with our books propped up in front of us, testing each other on the intricacies of the central nervous or digestive system and the prescribed treatment for a variety of ailments.

Much of our time was taken up by Sister Anne-Marie. She was studying for her finals by the time I had completed my first year, and was struggling with the amount she had to memorize. On the day of her hospital exams, she arrived home in tears and, at recreation, explained that she had left out a huge section relating to some aspect of postoperative care.

Sister Margaret, who was a great believer in interaction between earth and heaven, declared: "Don't worry, Sister. I shall have a special word with St Jude" (the patron saint of hopeless cases).

"Come on, Sister," said Sister Elizabeth tartly. "Either Sister Anne-Marie put it on her paper and she has forgotten in the stress of the moment, or she didn't. St Jude can't insert it miraculously into the text between now and next week when the paper is marked."

"He can if he so wishes," was the riposte.

When Sister Anne-Marie's paper was returned with a mark of over 70 per cent and the believed missing answer was there in all its detail, that good sister declared triumphantly, "You see, Sister Elizabeth, you have no faith. It has been put in."

"But not by me," grinned Sister Anne-Marie, always happy to stir. Sister Elizabeth only raised her eyebrows.

"I shall be very pleased," said Sister Catherine, "when Anne-Marie has taken her finals and we are no longer overwhelmed with all this drama." We settled down together to the complexity of the study of the skeletal system.

Occasionally I felt very claustrophobic in Mary-Mount. One day, needing fresh air, I found Mother Henrietta in the greenhouse with Sister Mary and bad-tempered Bijou.

"How's it going?" Mother asked, pinching the shoots out of the tomato plants, and looking keenly at me. "You look very tired sometimes."

"I love it, I really do. You were right, Mother; it's absolutely the thing for me, but it's a tiring job."

"It's not a job." Sister Mary's interjection was vehement. "You sound like an employee."

"I am employed by the hospital, so I suppose that makes me an employee."

"No! *Wrong*." She sounded incensed, even angry, and I felt my hackles rise. If I had been Bijou, I would have growled. "They didn't recruit you. We *sent* you there to train to be a nurse for the benefit of the congregation. The fact that they pay you is irrelevant. When you finish your training, you will leave the hospital."

"I don't know what you'll do with me. We can't all go to Lisdoonvarna or Porthmadog [we had small nursing homes there]. There's not enough for us to do. Don't you think it might be a good thing for the congregation to have a presence in a big general hospital?"

I felt I was addressing this question to Mother Henrietta and I w ished I were on my own with her. She looked thoughtful but was silent and I looked from one to the other. I wasn't sure quite who I was having this conversation with or what authority Sister Mary had to be so certain of my future.

"There has never been any question of the sisters working in a hospital," Sister Mary insisted with some vehemence.

"They do in France. The General Hospital in Le Mans doesn't belong to the congregation: it's state owned."

"We do have a convent in the grounds. The sisters pop back and forth easily," said Mother Henrietta mildly.

"So we are talking about geographical proximity: the difference between a hundred yards and four miles, and not whether nuns can work in state hospitals or not!"

"We've got plenty of time to decide what to do about you," she replied. Then glancing at Sister Mary she added with a chuckle, "Actually, the money they pay you" – I sensed she was reluctant to use the word "salary" – "is by no means irrelevant. See how unworldly Sister Mary is. It is extremely important."

Later that evening I commented to Sister Elizabeth, "Sister Mary seems very perky these days."

This was met with an ironic smile. "I expect she's practising."

"For what?"

"Sister Superior's term expires very soon."

"You think Sister Mary will be the new Superior? She's very young."

"Not that young. She's made final vows; she's eligible. Who else? They are not going to bring in somebody new here; the set-up is far too cosy."

I pretended to be shocked at her cynicism, but on reflection I recognized the possibility.

And she was quite right. Sister Mary was named Superior and things went on as before. I was quite pleased. I liked Sister Mary and, in the main, we got on well. She had a sharp tongue but was lively and energetic, with a good sense of humour, and took her responsibilities seriously. She was another nun who could have done so much more, given the opportunity. Being Mother's "secretary" allowed her small use of her undoubted ability. I am not sure what she did do; she certainly couldn't type. She was more Mother's "minder". She seemed to live her life through others;

their success was hers and any failure she took as a personal blow. Some of the community found her difficult, brusque, even harsh. She could be very dogmatic and lacking in empathy, but as she had always been Mother Henrietta's mouthpiece, there was no real change in the organizational life of the community.

I was never one of the little "in crowd" of sisters who orbited Mother, ran messages for her, and seemed to be at her beck and call, but despite that, I felt she and I were close and she often summoned me, flatteringly, to ask my opinion on something.

"Look at this," she said to me once, her voice trembling with indignation. "Mrs Kennedy has married Aristotle Onassis. She's a Catholic, for goodness' sakes, and he's a divorced man! What do you think?"

"Clearly she hasn't married him for his looks!"

"Good heavens, no," interjected Sister Mary, our new Sister Superior. "After Jack, imagine waking up to that raddled old head on the pillow beside you."

"Yes, but she has been used to a high-status position, Mother; to power, money, and influence. It can't be easy to give that up," I pointed out.

Mother Henrietta was not convinced. Sighing, she said, "But how can she, a Catholic, marry a divorced man? Surely she faces, if not excommunication, at least very heavy censure? In the eyes of the church, her marriage cannot be valid."

Sister Mary interjected sourly, "Wealthy Catholics seem to be able to get away with a great deal more than your ordinary run-of-the-mill ones. He's Greek Orthodox; maybe it makes a difference."

Mother Henrietta sighed again. She was genuinely disappointed, believing that the great, if not the good, had an obligation to show proper example to others. Alas!

Mother Henrietta had been equally perturbed by the appalling newspaper reports covering the ghastly crimes of the Moors Murderers and was at some pains to shield the older members of the community from the grimmer revelations, fearing that it would cause them too much distress. She insisted, however, with some vehemence that we pray for "all of them, even the dreadful perpetrators of such hideous crimes". I was impressed by her genuine Christian reaction, and my opinion of her as an unusual and admirable woman was reinforced.

Around that time I began to have increasing worries about my mother, and my new Superior was particularly kind. My parents' marriage was clearly at breaking point. The situation had deteriorated steadily since my return to England. My mother had been hospitalized on more than one occasion and my father was not a man to cope with the stigma, as it was then, of having a wife in a psychiatric hospital.

Then unexpectedly, early one morning, my brother, Peter, turned up. He had hitch-hiked from Portsmouth, arriving in Liverpool at about 4:00 a.m., only to discover he could remember neither my address nor the name of the congregation. He phoned Mount Pleasant, the teacher-training college, remembering that "Mount" figured in my convent's name. Grudgingly they gave him the telephone number for Mary-Mount and he slept in a phone-box until it was a reasonable hour to arrive on our doorstep.

I still had to go in to the hospital that day, so left him in the tender care of the community. He was very handsome and charming, and the older sisters fussed around him, fed, and watered him, so that when I got home that evening I found him ensconced like a lord, in the big parlour, eating supper with what looked like a glass of beer beside him.

"Who gave you that?"

"Bought it myself this afternoon. I didn't think I'd get any here."

"You'll ruin my reputation!"

"They didn't seem to mind – thought it was quite a joke."

"What are you doing here? Is anything wrong at home?"

"It's terrible at home." He looked young and frightened, probably because he was. "If they split up, I don't know what I'm supposed to do. Where am I going to live?"

He returned to Portsmouth the way he'd come. I felt very wretched about the whole situation and eventually Mother

Henrietta gave me compassionate leave to go home and see if I could help.

The visit was a disaster. My mother was clearly very ill. She overwhelmed me when we were alone together with tales of my father's alleged cruelty and infidelity, allegations that he denied vehemently. I was sure he was unkind and selfishly indifferent to her condition; I was less convinced about her accusations regarding the women. She showed signs of delusion, insisting that the woman next door was invading the house at night and leaving traces of lipstick and worse on the sheets. There were moments when she seemed more her old, sweet, bright, witty self, but they were rare. There was absolutely nothing I could do, so after several days I returned, depressed and anxious, to Liverpool, to my community, who drew me in and surrounded me with comfort, warmth, and prayer.

Over time, newly professed sisters continued to arrive at Mary-Mount, some for only a short time, others for longer. It made for a young, lively community, which was delightful, but it surprised me that nobody came to join us at Broadgreen. It was obvious that the work of the house was becoming harder for the older sisters. The entire responsibility for the catering fell on Sister Teresa's shoulders and it was not unreasonable that she should get some help, but it seemed a shame to see bright and vigorous young women spending their lives doing housework. Many of them eventually became extremely active in a variety of fields within the congregation, some studying abroad; but initially, indeed for years, they stagnated intellectually.

About this time we had a canonical visit from Reverend Mother General. I was genuinely pleased to see her; a breath of French air. She brought news from the Noviciate. My Sister Mistress of Novices had returned to St Julien, which must have delighted her, and had been replaced by a nun from Ma Maison, who had been a novice under the tutelage of Reverend Mother General and was considered a good and steady mentor for any aspirant to the religious life. But she didn't stay long. Sometime later, one bright day or possibly one night, she absconded abruptly, together with another sister to whom she had become very close – a case of a "particular friendship" that had become very particular indeed.

We all had a chance to see Reverend Mother General privately; she was friendly and seemed pleased that I was happy nursing. I was very tempted to ask about my future but knew she would refer me back to Mother Henrietta. She got a little frosty when I said I didn't think the new habit any improvement on the old. Our neat pleated black dress had been replaced with a grey under-dress covered by a long semi-fitted tunic. Our white collars, which were in fact a soft plastic and therefore very easy to clean, had been replaced by a sort of dicky front in some synthetic material. The new habit was no more washable than the old one had been.

She hadn't asked me my opinion; I had volunteered it and I think she was getting tired of hearing this sort of complaint.

"Fortunately," she said testily, "you weren't asked to make the decision about the change."

I didn't like to tell her that we were so disenchanted with our new outfit that some of us were already beginning to plan some changes to it.

She stayed about a fortnight, undoubtedly fortified with a sturdy English breakfast. Within days of her departure several of us, with Mother Henrietta's unexpected approval, were taking scissors to the hems of our dresses. We were not very daring – our dresses came on average to the bottom of our calves – although one hardy over-enthusiastic soul found herself with a dress that only just covered her knees. It was hardly mini-length but it was disapproved of all the same. Slowly, over the next few years, there was a wholesale, almost personal, adaptation of our clothes. Finally the habit became optional and many sisters eventually abandoned it altogether.

One of the changes that affected some of us more than others was the provision of a small sum of money. We had never had any spending money except in exceptional circumstances – a charity bazaar, for example. Sisters who needed travel expenses were given them; money was provided for shopping for shoes, underwear or things we needed for our work or study, but we had no personal income. So to be suddenly awarded ten shillings (in today's value about £5) a week and to be told we could spend it as we liked was more than startling.

This was a decision taken by Reverend Mother General and her Council. Nuns were sometimes accused of naïvety over the everyday problems of budgeting, so it was felt that the sisters should have personal experience of it. For some of us, this new departure was exciting, but for the older nuns, who in the main never left the house and who had last browsed the shops probably thirty years previously, the money was troublesome and even troubling. Having everything provided, wanting for nothing, they couldn't think what they would possibly want to buy or where to go if they did.

The situation was almost ludicrous. We were not allowed to accumulate the money. Anything unspent had to be given back at the end of the week and a fresh ten shillings given out. If none of it had been spent, the amount was returned intact into Sister Superior's hand and she then passed it back, or rather, in order to maintain the illusion that each week every nun received a fresh amount, Sister Margaret's unspent note was swapped for Sister Bernadette's unspent note. It was one of those convoluted rituals so common in convents at the time.

I bought a daily newspaper and an occasional paperback, only to discover that, as this was my personal shopping, I couldn't leave them lying around in the community room. Nuns, I was told repressively by my new, youngish Sister Superior, were not supposed to read newspapers. If I chose to buy one, she couldn't stop me but she could stop me offering it to others.

My boldest and secret purchase was tampons. I would have avoided a great deal of fuss if I had been open about this but I think, deep down, I knew it would have been disapproved of, so I suppose my omission was a fault against obedience. My purchase went undiscovered for several months and then someone became aware of it and reported me. The outraged reaction to this discovery was monumental. For Sister Superior, and inevitably for Mother Henrietta, this was tantamount to a serious fault against the vow, never mind the virtue, of chastity. My protests that millions of women were using them, and that there was absolutely no sexual aspect involved, only added fuel to the flame. Nuns are not other women: they do things differently, I was told, as if I didn't know.

"It's not as if we were in France," said Sister Superior. "I could understand you wanting something different. But here we have a cupboard full of sanitary towels! If it got out that a nun was using these things, people would assume you weren't..." She paused. "Well – you know."

"It just so happens that I'm not... Well – you know; but that is all in the past. I can't undo that, but today I am a nun bound by a vow of chastity and the use or non-use of tampons has got absolutely nothing to do with that." I was failing to convince her. Moved by her genuine distress and horror, I began to try to both comfort and reassure her.

"Sister Superior, if you don't want me to use them, I shall of course stop straight away. It is very unimportant to me; quite a small thing."

She began to calm down, saying she would take advice and talk to Mother Henrietta about it. And I did not hear another word on the matter. She neither forbade me to use them nor approved, so I carried on buying them.

CHAPTER 26

The Burns Unit and a Child Called David

Broadgreen had no children's unit, so for our paediatric experience we went to Alder Hey for eight weeks. This grim Edwardian building was in the improbably named Knotty Ash area of Liverpool, made famous by resident Ken Dodd. Even in the sixties the hospital enjoyed a formidable reputation for cutting-edge treatments and not just in surgery.

To my great satisfaction, my first ward was the burns unit. This small experimental ward had been designed, I was told, by a team of researchers who were looking to identify where and in what conditions burns healed quickest and best, and came up with Baghdad! So they attempted to replicate the climatic conditions prevalent there. It catered for about eight children. This was the only ward where I was not instantly identifiable as a nun. The unit was entered through an airlock where we changed into cotton shirts and trousers called "scrubs" and covered our head with paper caps. I thought it inadvisable to let Sister Superior know that I was "*sans* habit", as I thought she might make a fuss, so kept quiet about it.

Inside the unit it was hot and steamy. The children were nursed naked or very nearly, the slightly older boys with modesty pants. Their injuries, even the relatively minor ones, were horrendous. One small three-year-old, Debra, was minus an ear, a hand, most of her nose, eyelids, and a good part of her scalp. She had tumbled head first into a bucket of scalding water. The contraction from the subsequent scarring left her looking like a small malevolent alien. The majority of the patients were very young, some mere toddlers. Most of the injuries had been caused by the children pulling things down on top of themselves or falling onto or into fire or scalding water, so most had burns to the head, face or torso, a few to the buttocks.

If a large area of skin was damaged, the children were nursed not in bed but on non-stick silk mesh mattresses. Once their condition was stabilized, the raw areas were covered with postage-stamp grafts. Thin layers of skin were taken from areas of undamaged flesh, usually the thigh or buttock, and cut into small squares before being placed like patchwork over the wounds. The narrow areas between the grafts healed by a natural process called granulation. Then the whole area was covered with gauze impregnated with soft paraffin.

At first the grafted area looked good, a vast improvement on the dreadful sight beforehand, but as the area healed, the grafts shrank and the areas between contracted. The scarring that resulted was appalling. To keep all areas as soft and pliable as possible, the children were oiled with liquid paraffin. This made them as slippery as fish to deal with, something they learned very quickly. When they wanted to evade us, it wasn't difficult for them literally to slip between our fingers. The grafts were very fragile and easily scratched off or damaged if a child was lifted carelessly.

The trauma that these small children suffered, not just from the pain (although that was considerable), but from prolonged separation from their parents in such an unfamiliar environment, must have been unimaginable. Yet their behaviour gave the lie to all that. They were as naughty, sweet, funny, mischievous, disobedient, loving, uncooperative, obstinate, and demanding as any normal children, and we treated them as such. Even sick children can be spiteful and if they had squabbled, they often taunted each other with real or imaginary procedures that might be uncomfortable. Debra was particularly malicious.

"You're going in the bath today," she would say gleefully to another child due to have her dressings soaked off in a warm saline bath. It was actually quite a soothing procedure – some of the children even fell asleep – but they all lived with the likelihood of pain, so this sort of taunt always provoked tears.

"You are a naughty little girl. Go and say sorry at once," I scolded. She did so, reluctantly and begrudgingly, then she hung her head and huge tears dripped from her gaping damaged tear ducts. I pulled her onto my knee and put my cheek down onto her terrible scarred head, comforting and soothing her. What had this tiny creature ever done to merit such a catastrophic accident?

"Don't talk to me about guardian angels," I said furiously to Sister Margaret the next time she brought them up. She was a great fan of those nebulous entities. "That one must have been on her coffee break when her charge went headfirst into the boiling water!" Then I saw I had hurt her and felt ashamed yet again of my rash intemperate tongue.

It was in the burns unit that I first heard the magical music of the Beatles. The Mersey Sound must have been at its apogee in the mid-sixties. Having left Cliff Richard behind with "Livin' Doll" in 1960, the closest I got to pop after that was the sentimental and trivial songs of a Dominican nun, Soeur Sourire, or the ubiquitous Val Doonican. Mother Henrietta had more than a soft spot for Ken Dodd singing the "Barcarolle" but it was hardly rock and roll.

The burns unit had its own little operating theatre for primary grafting and one of the surgeons liked to work with background music. I was put in charge of the record player and handed three or four LPs. As wafer thin strips of skin were peeled off tender flawless thighs, and flayed flesh covered with a dermal patchwork, the songs and music of the Fab Four echoed incongruously round the little theatre. I fell desperately and instantly in love with all of them.

I was a month on the burns unit and then did a stint on an isolation ward. This was a very different kind of nursing, with each child alone in their glass cubicle. Some were very ill indeed with the childhood complaints that we see so rarely nowadays. A six-month-old baby boy was brought in, motionless, limp and grey, and looking moribund already. A lumbar puncture produced a thick opaque fluid and the laboratory report revealed pneumococcal meningitis. He got a shot of penicillin straight into the spinal cord and an antibiotic drip. An hour later, pink of body and puce-faced with rage, he was screaming his head off. "Well," said my Ward Sister with grim satisfaction, "don't you look a lot better!" He made a swift and total recovery. Many were not so lucky.

Nowadays, modern obstetrics and scans allow diagnosis of most foetal abnormalities very early. Then, these were rarely picked up during pregnancy and in any event there was very limited treatment for children afflicted with defects to the central nervous system. Pregnant women in their forties were sometimes offered tests on amniotic fluid which could alert them to Down's syndrome, and those with diabetes or a family history of it were prepared for possible complications, but with clinical abortion still very circumscribed, even abnormality was not automatically a reason for termination.

The isolation wards were full of seriously ill infants, including those with varying degrees of spina bifida, some complicated with hydrocephalus and gastrointestinal defects, sometimes complicated by infection. Hare lip and cleft palate were not uncommon. They needed intense, careful, and complicated nursing. I was a long way away from the cheerful general surgical wards of Broadgreen.

At the far end of the ward, I found David. He was a large baby, about eight months old, beautiful, and damaged. There was no external sign down his back of the devastating deformation of his spinal cord but his huge head was indicative enough. He was a quiet baby, and when he did cry, his soft wails were plaintive rather than demanding. A sad grandmother came to see him, sitting silent and puzzled beside his little cot. Sometimes she would pat his chubby little arm awkwardly. Did she hope he would recover?

"I think he's a little better today, Sister," she would sometimes say earnestly to me; or, "I think he's getting to know his old nan."

Whatever activity was going on inside David's head, it seemed to me that cognisance wasn't involved. He was not initially one of the infants allocated to my care but on night duty we dealt with all the children. I had to be careful picking him up to feed him, as the huge heavy head had to be supported. For the most part he was flaccid in my arms, but because of his condition he was very prone to fitting, so sometimes his small body was contorted with convulsions. Then his eyes would roll and his limbs, usually so floppy, would tense and contract. His cerebral turmoil was always silent.

I became deeply attached to him. Above his forehead he was monstrous, but from his straight dark eyebrows down he was perfect. His eyes, when he opened them (which he did infrequently), were a deep dark brown. His little body was like a plump Bernini cherub, his skin like milky opal. I got into the habit of talking to him when I fed and changed him, feeling he had the right to tenderness and to a demonstration of human contact. Although I knew his sensory abilities were virtually non-existent, I used the language of love and attachment and reassurance, the age-old phrases that mothers use to their babies; "Hello, my little poppet, are you hungry? Just let me get you out of this horrid wet nappy, then you can have your nice bottle. There, isn't that nice?" I stroked and tickled and caressed him as anyone would any child. He was completely unresponsive and a sluggish feeder, needing a lot of encouragement to finish a bottle.

Such was my feeling for him and my emotional involvement with him that I began to hope, ridiculously, that by some miracle he would be healed, and I asked the community to pray for him. Sister Superior didn't refuse but she obviously and probably correctly felt it was inappropriate.

"You should be more detached. You can't get this involved with your patients," she said severely.

It was sweet Sister Bernadette, "Bernie", who suggested gently that we should be praying for a swift end to his suffering.

"I am sure he knows you care for him," she said.

Next evening he fitted badly when I moved him, so it took me some time to change him, but he calmed down once he began to take his bottle. His head was terribly heavy against my arm and I propped my elbow up against the cot. In shifting him, I looked down. I was astonished to see his eyes were wide open, looking up unblinkingly at me. He let the teat slip out of his mouth and a trickle of milk slid down his cheek. He stared up at me as if he had known me for a very long time. It was a look of extraordinarily intense concentration. I stroked his cheek gently with my forefinger.

"Hello, David," I said and then, unbelievably, he gave a long, slow, sleepy smile and closed his eyes again.

"It was wind or another sort of fit."

"Oh yes, almost certainly." I wasn't going to argue with my Ward Sister when I heard her response.

"What do you think, Bernie?" I asked when I got home in the morning.

"I don't know, my dear; let's just hope he knew you." Then she added, "Our Lady will take him into her arms when he dies, and he will be perfect and beautiful and loved for all eternity. I am sure then that he'll know you loved him here on earth. Have you had your breakfast yet?" She was always eminently practical.

David died during my nights off, from the results of persistent fitting, status epilepticus, his tiny heart unable to cope. Self-indulgently, I allowed myself to cry for him, my face buried in the fluffy white nappies piled in the linen cupboard. His cubicle was not empty long. I thought of him for a long time afterwards and even now the memory of that unexpected and unbelievable milky smile still touches me like a blessing.

After my time at Alder Hey I made my annual retreat and, in May renewed my vows again happily. I still enjoyed and participated in community life. There is no doubt though that I was beginning to attach as great an importance to my work at the hospital as to my life in the convent, and it was a constant struggle to reconcile the two.

CHAPTER 27

Ghastly Gynae!

Our training as third-year students brought us to some other specialities. I prayed seriously that I would be spared gynaecology because of the fearsome reputation of the Ward Sister, Sister Thomas. Some student nurses were sent to Broadgreen's small maternity unit instead. Sister Anne-Marie did maternity rather than gynae but fate was against me and I was sent to gynae to face my nemesis.

Short, stout, and bandy-legged, immaculately uniformed, starched beyond belief, she inspired fear and apprehension in everyone. The housemen, whom she treated with withering contempt, were terrified of her; the registrars, whom she tolerated, were cautious; even the consultants were consciously respectful. The hospital porters, arriving to transport patients to X-ray or theatre, had to knock on the ward door and wait to be admitted like unwanted visitors. Elsewhere they breezed in expected but unannounced.

It was said that she detested both black nurses and Roman Catholics, so the gentle Ugandan nuns, I thought, were likely to have a rough ride. As she resented any change in routine, new nurses arriving on her patch were greeted with an aggressively unpleasant detailed explanation of her expectations. She made it quite clear that whatever standards we had met on other wards, hers were both more rigorous and better, and that she expected them to be adhered to.

She had particular non-nursing rituals that definitely set her apart. At 3:30 p.m. in the afternoon, when every other ward in the hospital was cheerfully dispensing tea from a huge pot on a large trolley, the gynae ward received sliced bread, butter, and jam, meat paste, or cucumber, together with a selection of Crawford's biscuits and paper napkins. One of the nurses was directed by Sister Thomas to set up individual tea trays with personal teapots, together with milk and sugar, and to make dainty sandwiches and serve them carefully to those patients able to enjoy them.

Occasionally large bunches of flowers were delivered to the ward. The staff nurse explained that they were from the crematorium. These funereal tokens, to my knowledge, never went to any other ward and I can only speculate how Sister Thomas acquired them and what sort of arrangement she had with the staff of that gruesome place. In the sluice room she would dismember the sheaves and reassemble them into smaller bunches, which she would distribute graciously to the nursing staff with a sort of grim smile. I would toss mine into the nearest rubbish bin on my way out, making sure she didn't see me!

She would have made an excellent dictator, having all the attributes of tyranny: enjoyment and abuse of power, contempt for her subordinates, a certain ruthlessness, a total belief in her own values, and an arbitrary disposal of her favour. She wielded her authority with cold, almost sadistic, enjoyment. She found fault with positive relish, liking nothing better than to reduce people to quivering uncertainty and apprehension. She would keep you waiting sometimes for an hour or more, full of anxiety, in order to censure you for some fault or failing that she had detected.

"Did you do so and so this morning? I see, well, go for your break. I'll talk to you about it when you get back." This guaranteed, as she well knew, a stomach-churning thirty minutes while you went over and over again in your head what you might have missed, done or not done. Once, I thought I had outwitted her when she played this unkind little game with me.

"I've got a half-day this afternoon, Sister, and I'm off tomorrow, so would you tell me now?"

"I'll see you about it when you are next on duty, Nurse Stewart," she replied, with an icy little smile.

"It is just maliciousness, but it's very nerve-racking. I can tell you, Sister Superior, she is the least Christ-like person I have ever had to deal with. Are you sure she was 'made in his image and likeness'?" I said, quoting the catechism. I was still churning with fury by the time I got home. My description of this repulsive woman had caused both shock and dismay in the community, mainly, I fear, because as a nun I was expected to try and see the best in everybody. The six or seven weeks I spent on the gynae ward were a constant struggle against antipathy.

Sister Thomas was technically an excellent nurse. The ward was spotless, her patients well cared for, and she was as hardworking as any of her staff. Once the night report had been given, her starched cuffs came off, her sleeves were rolled up, and she was out and about distributing medication, making beds, and organizing the work with military precision.

Astonishingly gentle and even tender with some "deserving" patients, she was vile to those who fell under the shadow of her moral judgment. Patients who had suffered an incomplete miscarriage were admitted to us because they needed a trip to theatre for a D&C. If the women were married, she was all sympathy, but if they were single, she made no attempt to hide her disapproval. Furthermore, she tended to believe that the miscarriages were all self-induced and when it was clear in some instances that that was indeed the case, the sad and frightened young women were treated with shameful contempt and open opprobrium.

One pathetic and simple-minded girl was so limited in her general ability that she couldn't keep herself clean, and her bed, apart from being bloodstained, was smeared with faeces. With a snort of disgust, our repellent Ward Sister whipped the sheet from the bed, hissing, "This is *quite* unnecessary; you should be ashamed of yourself!"

The wretched girl stared at the bed with bemusement, clearly puzzled as to the provenance of the stain, and then said slowly, "Where did that come from? I don't think I done that. What's all that mess?"

"Where do you think it's come from? It's you, of course."

This interaction took place in an open ward and even some of the other patients were clearly perturbed by it.

"Don't frighten her, Sister, she's a poor little thing," called out one of them.

Emboldened by this, I volunteered, "I'll take her to the bathroom, Sister. I'm sure she will be happier when she's had a little wash."

She had the grace to be silent and turned from me with a pinched mouth.

She got what she thought was her revenge a few days later when a woman was admitted who needed isolation nursing.

"I've got a nice little job for you, Nurse Stewart!"

A pale thin woman was wheeled into the single room at the far end of the ward. I stood at the end of the bed while the medical team examined her. When she parted her thighs, I saw that the entire vulva looked as if it were covered with white carnations. She groaned with pain.

"Herpes, but also a secondary infection here," said the registrar. "Antibiotics for that and analgesia, and Savlon washes as often as she wants. Do you think you can manage that?" He turned to me.

"Don't touch another patient while she's here!" My Ward Sister's directive was actually welcome, as it meant that as long as I was nursing this unfortunate patient, I was spared any interaction with the rest of the ward. For the next few days, every twenty minutes, I poured warm soothing lotion over the inflamed and infected area, and very rapidly the hideous flowering reduced.

We had long friendly conversations about her family in County Sligo and her little girl, Maeve.

"They think I'm married and work in an office, you know. I learned to type when I left school, then I got pregnant and came to Liverpool. Couldn't tell them at home; they'd have sent me to the nuns and taken the baby away. Anyway, I couldn't get a job in an office because of the baby, and I had a friend who said it was easy money, no one would know at home, and I could do it for a short time till I got some cash together. I'm sure my Mammy knows about me, but what can I do? Then I got this. I didn't know what it was at first, but it got so bad so quickly. In the end I went to the doctor. He wanted to know the names of the men I'd been with but I couldn't remember. Anyway they always give false names. I'm so ashamed that you should see this; I say my rosary every day, you know."

"Don't be silly. It's an infection like any other infection." I calmed and comforted her, and poured endless jugs of Savlon over her.

Surprisingly, the Ward Sister, never one to praise when she could censure, said grudgingly that I'd done what she called a "good job". She tempered this compliment with criticism about the dust on the windowsill.

My patient was discharged with stern admonishments from this dour woman about never having sex again unless her partner wore a condom. Without one, she was likely to infect them all.

"What am I supposed to tell a future husband, should I ever be lucky enough to find one?" was the riposte.

I saw her over a year later, on the bus, with a pleasant-looking man. Her little girl was on his knee and she had a small baby in her arms. They looked happy and relaxed. She saw me and, to my astonishment, greeted me. Usually patients with embarrassing complaints not unreasonably failed to recognize the nurses who had looked after them. Her husband, for so he turned out to be, said, "She's always talking about you, Sister, and how you looked after her. Look, here's our little boy. He's a month old now."

What she told him, God knows. There were so many "maybes". Maybe she had told him the truth and he loved her anyway; maybe the virus would never reoccur; maybe it would often reoccur, maybe... maybe... maybe.

I finished my six weeks on the gynae ward and my place was taken by Sister Catherine. She got on astonishingly well with

Sister Thomas. I attributed this to my companion's sunny, cheerful, hardworking temperament. I think she drew out from that seriously unpleasant woman some hidden but better part of her nature. Sister Catherine was the most willing and sweet-natured nun I ever met. I never heard a harsh, sour, or unkind word from her, and to my shame I think she suffered from my sometimes brusque, inquisitorial manner.

On one of the rare weekends when I wasn't at the hospital, Mother Henrietta took me aside and asked me if I would talk to the sisters about birth control. She felt they ought to know what was involved. The papal encyclical *Humanae Vitae* was not promulgated until 1968 but there was a great deal of discussion going on about contraception. The church was in a ferment of angst about it and it was widely believed, erroneously as it happened, that there would be some concessions made, because the pill was viewed by many Catholics as being quite acceptable.

I was aghast at Mother Henrietta's request!

"Can't I bring some pamphlets home, Mother? Do I have to talk to them about it?"

"Bring pamphlets home and *then* talk to the community."

They all listened very politely and asked a few sensible questions. The other more mechanical methods – intrauterine contraceptive devices, the Dutch cap, and condoms – they thought distasteful. They were disgusted by withdrawal and it was generally agreed that tubal ligation was too final, but they were universally in favour of the contraceptive pill, which they agreed was efficient and non-invasive. When I said that the rhythm method was the only one allowed by the church, they looked at each other in silent bewilderment.

CHAPTER 28

More Night-time Drama and that "Lovin' Feeling"

Thoracic surgery was an umbrella term for any surgery of the chest cavity. Cardiac surgery would normally be a separate category, but in Broadgreen, at that time, we had no separate ward for patients who returned from the intensive therapy unit following open heart surgery. Generally, if they made it back to the ward they were going to recover. Surgery for lung or oesophageal cancer was more problematic. Sometimes, following an exploratory operation, the cancer was found to be inoperable and patients would be told, "We've done what we can for you. You should make a good recovery from the operation and when you are all healed, you'll be able to go home." This was true, but disguised the real situation. Some didn't make it that far and I saw a lot of death on the thoracic wards, some very ghastly indeed.

Pain control, as we understand it today, was unknown in the sixties. Following surgery, patients were routinely prescribed two four-hourly injections of an opiate (very exceptionally they got a third one) and that was pretty well it. This was usually but ineffectually followed by oral analgesia, so severe postoperative pain was the norm. Those with intractable pain were dosed with a sinister concoction called Mist Euphorians, which consisted of gin, honey, and oral morphine. It was useless.

Patients considered suitable for radiotherapy were transferred to another hospital. A few were subjected to chemotherapy; both these treatments were fearsome. Sometimes you longed for a patient to die but it was astounding how long that process could take. Time after time I would arrive on duty convinced that some desperately ill patient would have had the grace to die in the night, only to find them, increasingly emaciated and sunken-eyed, sometimes barely lucid but clinging grimly and determinedly to life. In Mary-Mount they were always praying for a rapid and peaceful end for someone.

"Don't any of your patients recover?" asked Sister Margaret crossly one evening at recreation.

"Yes, but I'm not likely to ask you to pray for the ones that are getting better, am I!"

All the nurses, particularly at night, were, as I have said, the reluctant recipients of confidences that they would rather not have heard. The outpourings of personal anxieties and intimacies often followed an alleviation of physical discomfort, as if the emotional release was triggered by a corporal solace. A quiet, reserved fifty-year-old woman from Wrexham in North Wales came in for a repair of a hiatus hernia. This was a serious operation involving both the chest and the abdominal cavity. She seemed to make a good recovery and then, about five days after the operation, began to run a high temperature. She was prescribed antibiotics and we checked her wound nervously for signs of infection with the dreadful and dreaded bacterium *clostridium welchii*. Normally harmless in the gut, if it got into a wound it could cause gas gangrene, which in a debilitated patient is almost invariably fatal. There was none of the ominous crackling of the flesh around the incision that indicated its presence, so we moved her to a side ward, waited for the antibiotics to get to work, and monitored her carefully.

I found her wide awake and restless in the small hours. She looked grey and toxic, her skin dry and hot, her temperature above 40°C.

"I'm so sore and uncomfortable; my side hurts."

"Let's have a little look at you." I got a dressing pack, washed my hands, and cautiously removed the pad covering her wound.

The area was inflamed and the suture line had an ugly bluish tinge, and was oozing a little. One of the stitches had come loose and dropped onto the pad. I took a sinus forceps, a slender instrument for probing or packing a wound, and tentatively inserted it into the gap left by the stitch. Instantly about two inches of the bluish suture line opened and, like obscene language from a dirty mouth, a thick flood of foul-smelling grey-green pus began to gush out. The gauze and cotton wool swabs were quite inadequate to cope with it. I collected several sterile towels and went back to her bedside, turning her a little on her side. The pus flowed and flowed. There must have been half a pint of it.

"Oh my, that feels better; that feels so much better," she said gratefully. "Sorry about the mess!"

Waiting for the duty doctor, I sat beside her while she drank a cup of tea.

"I think this is a punishment from God," she announced. My heart sank as I recognized the preamble to a string of confessional disclosures.

"Mrs Bevan, I'm sure it isn't; it's an infection. I don't think God punishes us like this. I don't think God punishes us at all, actually."

"How can you say that? The Bible is full of God punishing people!"

It was three o'clock in the morning and, with the best will in the world, I didn't think I was up to an intellectual discussion with a sick woman on biblical exegesis. It was astonishing how many people felt illness was a punishment for sin. I began to understand why the, to my mind, dubious beliefs of the Christian Scientists were so credible to so many. But before I could say a word, and to my consternation, she began, gently, to cry.

"I haven't been well for ten or twelve years. There's been one thing after another." She paused, then added, "It's all to do with my insides! God's punishing my insides – that's how I know." If it weren't for the fact that her temperature by this time was nearly normal, I'd have thought her delirious.

"What do you mean, your insides?"

"I've been ill off and on but never with anything external, always inside: pain and discomfort, heartburn and terrible indigestion, bloating and constipation, not to mention disturbed nights. Never a rash or a broken arm or anything I could see."

"You were suffering from a hiatus hernia; these are all the symptoms." By this time, I could see she didn't want to be comforted or reassured. She was indulging in an orgy of psychological self-flagellation.

"Yes, but why did I get it? I'll tell you why. My husband was in the merchant navy. I was stupid. There was this young chap – beautiful he was and he made such a fuss of me. Well, anyway, I found I was pregnant. I knew it couldn't have been my husband's, he'd been away too long. So my friend knew this woman and I had an abortion. I never told my husband but I've felt guilty and ashamed ever since. What a thing to do – my one chance to have a child of my own. The worst of it is, I think he'd have forgiven me and loved the baby. He always said it was hard on a woman being on her own. He always wanted children. I just panicked, you see. It was done before I'd really thought about it. My insides haven't been right since and when I saw all that filth coming out of me, I knew I was right about God's punishment."

There was nothing I could say to persuade her she was mistaken, so I held her hand, patting it gently. I felt deeply sorry for her and sad that she should believe in such a malicious and frightening God.

"Well, she was clearly demented." Sister Superior's comment later back at Mary-Mount was brusquely unsympathetic, but other members of the community expressed some understanding.

"Guilt," said Sister Margaret, "often expresses itself in an odd way." There was a murmur of agreement. Did it help Mrs Bevan, I wondered, to believe she was being punished? Sadly, I felt it did.

As my third year of training unfolded, I became increasingly concerned about what was on the cards for me when I qualified. I believed it was counter-productive to ask Mother Henrietta directly, so one day out in the car with her I began to talk casually about the hospital, teasing her about her confidence in her favourite TV oracle.

"Well, Mother, Richard Dimbleby was wrong. Surgery is not bloodless. Theatre, I'm told, is awash with it."

She chuckled, and then threw the ball back to me. "So, you've got the theatre, intensive care, and Casualty, and then it's your finals. What next?" I thought it was a rhetorical question and so remained silent, hoping against hope that she wasn't going to say Ireland or Wales.

I took a deep breath and then risked saying, "I would very much like to do midwifery." Sister Anne-Marie had finished her general nursing training and started midwifery, and although I knew she was being considered for the African Province, she had set a precedent. Mother Henrietta didn't respond and I too was silent. I felt despondent and no further forward. We ended the journey in silence.

"Enjoy your theatre experience. That's next, isn't it? Oh, and not too many graphic details," she said, as we went into the house. "It upsets some of the community." Then she added, patting my arm, "Don't worry about the future," and she chuckled again.

Instead of praying for the humility to accept whatever my Superiors decided, I began to pray determinedly for my own desires to be fulfilled. Deep down, when I took a long hard look at my attitude, I knew this was not the correct spiritual mindset. I knew I should have enough confidence in God's plan for me to leave it, as it were, up to him. Once again obedience was a problem for me.

Contrary to my expectations, and despite the smart shininess of our new Honeywell Theatre suites, I found theatre dull, all the patients asleep or very nearly, the surgeons prima donna-ish, and the staff nurses and sisters stern. The insides of bodies may be fascinating but it is difficult to feel any personal empathy with a ruptured kidney or a perforated gastric ulcer. For student nurses, time in theatre seemed mostly housework, cleaning, washing instruments, or if you were in theatre during an operation, counting swabs to make sure one hadn't been left behind inside. It was important work but not very interesting.

Casualty, on the other hand, was vibrant, and there I think I fell in love, or at least felt the stirrings of something I thought I had put behind me forever. He was a tall and broad houseman with red hair and a cheerful freckled face. He made me laugh. There is undoubtedly something seductive about shared humour. One fairly quiet night we were passing around the local newspaper. Insensitive as ever, I began to read out some of the dreadful doggerel in the In Memoriam column, about "pearly gates" and "God only taking the best". I was laughing so loudly, I failed to notice the disapproving silence of my companions.

I was encouraged by my handsome houseman, who told us that in the agony column of another paper he had read recently, someone had advertised for a companion with possible marriage in mind, which finished "Cripples considered". When our joint laughter died down, the staff nurse said my attitude − that I should "mock the bereaved" − had astonished her. When I pointed out that these messages were picked out of a book and were not the painful efforts of individuals themselves, she said sharply that that didn't matter. I was, in her opinion, sneering at people's heartfelt endeavour to convey their feelings. Aware that I had caused some scandal, I subsided, but unfortunately caught the eye of my fellow mocker and had to retire to the sluice where, with a mixture of giggles and remorse, I tried to compose myself.

"It's OK," he said, following me in. "*I'm* not shocked."

"Why would you be? Your story was worse than any comments of mine. You made it up, didn't you?"

We stared smiling at each other and I thought, *Yes, I could certainly fall in love with you!*

When he wasn't on duty the shift seemed dull, and when he was and I first saw him, my mouth would become dry and I felt a breathless pounding behind my breastbone.

Sometimes I have been asked if I ever had *a thing* going with a doctor when I was a nursing nun. I have always said that any doctor who fancied a plump bespectacled nun, when there were hundreds of the prettiest mini-skirted young nurses around, would have been odd, not to say deviant, so the answer has to be: No, I never had a thing going, but I did find my houseman very attractive. I knew that I should speak to my Superiors about it, even though it was as innocent as could be. But I was almost certain that they would withdraw me from the hospital, and my commitment to nursing was, by now, as great as my commitment to my vows. In the event, the situation resolved itself. I worked hard and prayed to overcome what I was sure was just a sentimental attachment, and he went off to work in another department.

We did see some horrendous stuff in Casualty. The ambulance men, who were beyond praise, dealt with the immediate disasters. Unfailingly polite, cheerful, and above all competent, we all loved, admired, and respected them. Most fatalities couldn't be taken straight to the mortuary, as the death had to be certified. BID or DOA was scrawled on the notes: "Brought in dead" or "Dead on arrival". Sometimes they were so badly injured you wished they had been BID. One elderly man had been hit by a motorbike; he was carried in, his legs hidden in box splints. Chatty and cheerful, he reassured the doctor who lifted the covers.

"Oh God," gasped the registrar, staring down and unable to hide his horror. The lower legs were virtually severed through the tibia, the brutal raw ends of the bone red and white, clearly visible.

"It's not too bad, Doctor, is it?" He was in such shock he felt nothing. Miraculously he survived, but whether he walked again, I don't know.

Often in the space of an hour we went from the ghastly to the commonplace. On almost a daily basis we treated workmen with haematomas (a collection of blood) trapped beneath a finger nail, usually caused by a heavy hammer blow. It didn't look much but the pain was exquisite. The treatment was very basic. A paperclip was opened up and the end grasped in a locking forceps. The other end was heated with a lit match until the end was red hot. We asked the patient to put their finger flat on the desk, then burned through the nail with the red-hot paperclip. Sometimes the trapped blood spurted a foot high. Strong men fainted – not from the pain, which was instantaneous and over swiftly, but from the thought of what we were about to do! It was remarkably efficacious.

For all my imagined sophistication I remained extraordinarily naïve about real life. I had already been teased in my first year when I failed to recognize the pregnancy of a fellow student nurse and kept telling her she needed a firmer girdle. Patients coming into Casualty following a "domestic", as it was called, were horribly embarrassed by my innocent questions.

"Tea! How did he get burns from tea on the back of his neck?"

Dealing with injuries sustained by drunks was not difficult. The respect for nurses amounted almost to veneration. I never heard a nurse being abused or threatened. There was never any need for the warning notices, found today in A&E, alerting people about police intervention in the event of aggressive behaviour. Patients sometimes fought among themselves, but verbal insults and the odd thrown punch, usually ineffectual, was the extent of altercations.

One night, two large women of indeterminate age were brought in, one semi-conscious and the other with a black eye and a cut on her cheek. They were accompanied by their respective families. There seemed to be hundreds of them. It transpired there had been a shouting match through a letter box that culminated in a street fight.

"She called me mam a dirty old whore!" said an indignant son. "I grant you, Sister, she doesn't look too clean now, but she wouldn't do, now, would she? She's been rolled on the pavement by that slag there! She may be old but she's not a whore!"

"Don't be daft, mate," said the ambulance man, cheerfully heaving the snoring woman onto a couch. "You know she's been on the game for years; not that she deserves to be beaten up for it," he added hastily. I didn't envy the staff on the ward when this lady was admitted.

However, the following morning, apparently, the aggressor arrived with beautiful clean clothes to dress and escort her "friend" home. There were mutual tears of contrition and fulsome apologies to each other and to everyone else. Huge boxes of chocolates and flowers were brought in for the staff on Casualty and a large potted plant for the ward. I saw both of them with their families at Mass the following Sunday.

I had three tough weeks in the intensive therapy unit but faced no unexpected dramatic incidents, and then went into the final year study period before taking my exams. I knew that I had done well in the hospital exams and expected to get my state registration in January 1968. I had serious expectations of getting a hospital medal, gold, silver, or bronze, awarded to the best students, as throughout my training, my exam results had been excellent. I had also, so I'd been told, got good ward reports. Sister Superior had convinced herself that I would get the gold medal, awarded to the best nurse in final year, and as I did think I was in line for it, I didn't caution her as I should have done. On the day of the awards, I smiled bravely and congratulated the medal winners I hope with real warmth and sincerity. Sister Superior rushed back to Mary-Mount ahead of me and pulled down the congratulatory banner that had been erected in anticipation of my triumph. She was very bitter about the lack of a medal and I don't think she ever forgave me.

It was a salutary lesson and I think Mother Henrietta, with her usual perspicacity, got it right when, comforting me later in her office, said, "Never mind, Sister, it's only glory. We all know you are a good nurse." Then with an ironic little smile, she added, "Too much of this" – she touched her mouth – "gets you this," and she drew her hand across her throat. "*I* learned that many years ago!"

It was some compensation that I was finally given permission to do midwifery. I applied to the Liverpool Maternity Hospital and was accepted. I was sad to leave Broadgreen, but LMH was undoubtedly more prestigious and would give me wider experience.

CHAPTER 29

Midwifery, Three-Year Vows, and Uncertainty

LMH was in the city, close to the new Catholic Metropolitan Cathedral. The unusual shape of this building gave it its inevitable soubriquet of "Paddy's Wigwam". It was a beautiful building, filled with a pale translucent light coming from a circle of green glass windows high up, just below the funnel-shaped turret. It was like being underwater. The proximity to the hospital meant I had no problem getting to Mass. One Sunday morning I found myself next to Sir Alec Guinness. I always regretted not getting his autograph; Mother Henrietta would have loved it.

The rota at LMH was straightforward: two day shifts, 8:00 a.m. till 6:00 p.m. and 1:00 p.m. till 10:00 p.m., and then a night shift, 10:00 p.m. till 8:00 a.m. The lateness of the hours worried Mother Henrietta, who insisted I took taxis if I was arriving or leaving after dark. On public transport I often travelled free, the drivers either refusing my money or accepting my fare from another passenger. I would hear, "No, you keep your money, Sister," or "I'll pay for you, Sister; just say one for me." It was useless protesting.

I never stood on a bus either, always being offered a seat. I was pleased to accept one from a child, indignantly pushed upright by an insistent parent, or from a man. I was never feminist enough to put up with discomfort in the interest of equality. I was filled with embarrassment, however, when elderly travellers heaved themselves breathless and panting to their feet to offer me their place. I believed it was the nun's habit they were ceding their place to and not me, but it was difficult just the same.

As I had done at Broadgreen, I settled down happily. LMH seemed small and intimate and everybody knew each other; it was friendly. One or two nurses came from other hospitals in the city but most of my colleagues came from further south, drawn by the reputation of the hospital.

When you have trained somewhere for a considerable period of time, in a particular fashion, there is a tendency to think that there is one definitive way of doing something. So it was fun, if startling, to discover this was not so.

"Can you take the diabetic bloods for me, Sister?" one of the midwives asked me on my second day. Samples were needed for analysis. I was shocked.

"We were never allowed into a vein at Broadgreen," I said. A sassy, pretty red-headed pupil midwife called Sarah, from Coventry, cheerfully offered to show me how.

"Good God," she said, "you make it sound like being refused booze in a pub. *You can't come into this vein until you can prove that you are over eighteen.* Not that you'd know anything about that, Sister," she added hastily. She was so deft. I was astonished at how easy it looked, and got the hang of it quickly.

We were all longing for our first delivery but had to see ten normal ones first. When a mother was in second stage, actively pushing, a bell rang in all areas where pupils might be working. We dropped everything and rushed to the labour ward, so it was chaotic as we jostled to see what was going on. The mothers were amazingly sanguine about it all. Many had done it all before and would gasp between pushes, "Can you all see, girls?"

Thankfully, given the birth rate in Liverpool, it didn't take us long to clock up our ten witness deliveries and when eventually, with a midwife standing behind to guide and direct me, I delivered my first, and pulled that slippery, perfect creature into the world, I thought there was nothing that I would rather do in life. It was wonder and magic, it was messy and bloody and fantastic, and it seemed to me the greatest privilege imaginable.

Back at Mary-Mount there was a mixed reception to my excitement. Sister Superior, whose attitude to the physical was mainly revulsion, though she covered it well, shuddered at my sanitized description, then collared me after supper to warn me against giving any details relating to the hospital.

"We don't need to know the ins and outs of midwifery. What you do at the hospital stays at the hospital. The community doesn't need to know about childbirth and the newborn; it's inappropriate to talk about it."

"So," I replied tersely, "I can take my convent life to the hospital but I mustn't bring my hospital life home."

"That's right, and you don't have a *hospital life*. Your life is here. You just happen to work, at the moment, elsewhere." She emphasized "at the moment". I wondered what had become of the vivacious, witty, laughing woman I knew who had giggled with me about Richard Dimbleby and who had teased the costermongers in the market. There wasn't much fun about her now. She had changed over time, perhaps because she took her duties very seriously, but also I fear because authority had gone to her head a bit. She had become discouragingly humourless and stiff. On the other hand maybe she saw the way I was drifting. Resentment bubbled up in me, and yet again I had to bite my tongue.

Midwifery was not all sunshine and flowers; there were pregnancies that ended sadly: stillborn infants, malformations, and seriously premature babies, frail as a breath, that clung to life, sometimes hopelessly. Pregnancy wasn't good for everybody either. Some women were irremediably damaged by it, carrying the consequences of pre-eclampsia for the rest of their lives. Babies with rhesus positive blood, carried by rhesus negative mothers, were also gravely at risk. A pregnancy seriously compromised by the anti-rhesus factor almost inevitably ended in a dead baby. The few that were born alive might survive a blood transfusion but this was a delicate affair and some did not. For women who knew that the outcome was a dead or damaged baby, the wait was terrible and the labour fruitless.

Occasionally, Sister Elizabeth and I talked quietly together. She was doing her teaching practice and was also forbidden to talk about her day. I found myself more and more involved with people and situations outside my convent life. Resentment and frustration were building up, but this was not all; over and above the genuine pleasure in my work, I began to feel overwhelmingly what I can only describe as maternal yearning. I was surrounded by fecundity, babies in the womb, at the breast, in cots, on my knee, in my arms as I fed and changed and cuddled them. The longing for a child may well be natural and normal, but it is hardly concomitant with a vow of chastity.

In May I took my three-year vows and made this longer commitment with, for the first time, some hesitation, although the act itself was reassuring. For a few weeks afterwards I was calm and my spirit lightened. I had asked if I might renew my vows just for a further one year, rather than making the three year commitment, but was assured by both Sister Superior and Mother Henrietta that my uncertainty was natural and understandable. I had a busy life outside the community. When my training was finished and I was more "settled", all would be well. I was far from sure that I wanted to be settled, particularly if it meant a return to the seclusion of community life.

I had an unexpected visit from my father. The rule of no men overnight in the house meant finding other accommodation for him. Mother Henrietta recommended a small hotel in the city, run by a friendly Irish woman she vaguely knew, and we set off to find it. The room we were shown was windowless and, apart from the bed covered with rumpled sheets from the previous occupant and a wash basin, was unfurnished. My father looked at it in silence for a moment and then, with the utmost civility, said, "Thank you, but I think I need something closer to my daughter's convent."

Outside he turned to me. "Good God, darling, what the hell was Mother Henrietta thinking of? It's a knocking shop!"

"What! She'll never believe it. Mrs what's-her-name is a good, practising Catholic."

"She could be Pope Joan herself; she's running a brothel." He was more startled than shocked.

I think Sister Superior thought it was bad form of my father to have mentioned it and that he would have done better to save Mother's face and stay there, obviously carefully locking the door. Clearly the kind of man who could identify a brothel was a dubious sort anyway. I am afraid it was too good a story to keep to myself, so I shared it with some of my younger companions in community, who were convulsed with a mixture of horror and hilarity. One of them was unwise enough to comment laughingly on it to Sister Superior. As she could only have learned about it from me, this earned me a very serious reprimand.

My parents' marriage was clearly coming to an end. My father was defensive, but as my mother was hospitalized yet again and was therefore safe, I chose cravenly not to interrogate him too much. I did talk to him about my own frame of mind and he was supportive and sympathetic.

"If you want to leave, no one will reproach you. Eight years is a long time."

Said so bluntly this took my breath away, but from that evening, sitting talking to him in Mary-Mount's pleasant parlour, I began to envisage a life elsewhere. I thought it would be dishonest of me not to speak to my Superiors about my feelings, but bypassed Sister Superior and went directly to Mother Henrietta. By the time I plucked up courage to ask to see her, I was in a turmoil of uncertainty and confusion. She was unbelievably kind, gentle, sympathetic, and reassuring.

"You've been looking a bit peaky for some time now." This was a favourite expression of hers and covered everything from being a bit off colour to imminent demise.

"Do you want to go back to France? Would that be better for you?" Her concern was genuine and I was touched by her willingness to do whatever it took to help. I didn't think that it would make any difference, and I said so.

"I could," she said, "bring you back into community to do something else. You are much loved here; you are lively and make us laugh. It could help you, and the community would perhaps benefit from seeing more of you."

Eventually we agreed that overall it would be better for me to complete my diploma. If this was a test of my commitment to the religious life and just a passing fancy and, she stressed, a perfectly natural reaction to the environment in which I was working, then ultimately, better qualified, I would be more use to the congregation. Alternatively, she said bravely, if I decided that my path led elsewhere (I smiled tearfully at the euphemism), well then… She left the sentence incomplete. She suggested that I try to put the whole thing aside while I concentrated on my training; that I carry on as normal, fulfil my religious obligations, participate as much as possible in community life, and see how it went.

"I'll pray very hard for you," she said. I left her, comforted and very determined to "give it a go", as she suggested.

Part 2 of the midwifery diploma was district rather than hospital based. I was attached to a midwife on the verge of retirement who lived within walking distance of Mary-Mount. Her name was Sister Dawkins and she was lovely. Not unnaturally, she was a great believer in home births and never called the women in her care "patients", as this implied they were ill, which in the main they were not. They were "clients" or more often "mothers".

My midwife had a neat little car, which she drove with extreme caution and treated as if it were an animate creature. When she braked, she hauled back on the steering wheel as if reining in a horse. I always expected her to say "whoa". I am not sure if she ever felt in complete control of the vehicle and am sure she would have been happier with a pony and trap.

In the evening in her cosy little sitting room, when we had finished our rounds, she fed me tea and cream buns in front of the fire. For the first time since entering my convent, I spent time inside people's homes and realized what a sheltered existence I had led.

If my midwife's house was warm and cosy, I was disconcerted and dismayed by the state of many others. Some were neat and clean, but others were filthy beyond belief, the combination of poverty, poor health, and bad housing making often for a sort of passive resignation to life in general. Cleaning, I thought, would have needed a motivational effort, which was clearly lacking. On other occasions I met vigorous cheerfulness and a determination not to be ground down by the vicissitudes of life. There was an astonishing resilience in the face of repeated knock-backs. Liverpudlians were some of the most robustly optimistic people I had ever come across. They had warmth and a directness that was as endearing as it was disconcerting.

They could also be very obstinate. Women who had made up their minds about having their baby at home couldn't be budged, no matter what contra-indications arose. Consequently we were sometimes faced with extremely risky situations; a mother whose previous pregnancy had been complicated by hypertension refused transfer to hospital even though her blood pressure rose to alarming heights. We darkened the room and spoke in whispers in case our "mother" fitted.

When we were on night call I slept on a camp bed in the parlour as, apart from Mother Henrietta's office, the only other phone was in the hall. Birth, like death, seems to happen very often in the small hours, so it wasn't unexpected to be woken at 2:00 a.m. by the midwife's ever cheerful voice: "We're off, Sister; pick you up in ten minutes."

One dark moonless night we were called to a labouring mother in Princess Avenue, an elegant road with its central area of trees and sandy walks. The large merchants' houses had been split up into miserable little flats and bed-sits and the whole area, once so prosperous, was seedy and down at heel. We paused uncertainly outside a large unlit house; it looked almost derelict. We were covering for another midwife that night, so we knew neither the mother nor the area.

"Do you think this is it?"

The midwife consulted her notes. "Looks like it."

We pushed the front door hesitantly and went in; she flashed her torch and found a light switch. We were in a splendid, very large rectangular hall that rose up through two storeys to a glass roof. It was empty, apart from two old bicycles chained together, and a sack containing logs sitting in a puddle of water. It smelled damp. A broad elegant staircase led up to a galleried landing that ran around three sides of the hall. Numbers were coarsely painted on the beautiful oak doors. We found our client sitting up in bed, drinking a cup of tea and smoking a cigarette.

"I hope I haven't called you too early, but you have to go miles to find a bloody phone that works. The kids are with their dad at Sylvia's place, number 3."

The sheets were grubby but we always carried newspapers, working on the premise that clean newsprint was preferable to dirty bedding. Hundreds of babies must have been delivered on the inside sheets of the *Liverpool Echo*. She hadn't called us too early at all; twenty-five minutes later and still talking, she gave birth.

"Not another bleeding girl," she said cheerfully. "Never mind. Long as it's healthy." I went off to find her husband and he came back with me, carrying two sleepy little girls whom he deposited on the bed and who promptly fell asleep beside their mother. Neighbours crowded in. There must have been twenty or more, and the whole atmosphere became positively party-like and jolly. It was hard to believe this dark dank place housed so many exuberant people. Everybody brought something; one very bent old lady presented a bottle of stout. Our "mother" sat like a queen receiving them all, her baby at her breast.

"He works for a butcher," she said, nodding at her husband. "He'll make us some bacon butties soon, won't you, pet? We may be short of other things but we've always got meat." They certainly weren't short of happiness and contentment either; the bacon butties were good too.

On another occasion, late in the evening, we were called out to attend a mother living in the incongruously named "John Fitzgerald Kennedy Heights" on Everton Brow, one of the grim tower blocks set in a savage landscape that the city council had thought an improvement on the neat little artisan terraces that they had so enthusiastically demolished. The whole place had an air of desolation. In the dingy hall, with its odour of urine and vomit, I found my midwife. She was looking at a billboard advertising a play called *The Devil Came from Dublin*. Someone had scrawled across it in chalk "and settled here"! We smiled ruefully, then, sighing, she pointed. "Just our luck," she said, indicating the sign on the lift: OUT OF ORDER. "You go ahead of me," she added. "Your legs are younger than mine. Tell her I'm on my way."

I set off up the unlit stairs. Halfway up, with dread I heard the sound of scampering paws and flattened myself against the wall. My heart pounded as a small pack of feral dogs rushed past me. I'd met this sort of thing before. Even with shortened skirts, our habits drew them like a magnet. I'd been the object of the hostile attention of similarly unfriendly animals on other unpleasant occasions. They would circle, stiff legged, their hackles up, growling softly with their teeth bared. I dreaded a repeat. Thankfully, apart from one of them pausing to sniff suspiciously at me and then raising his leg against the graffiti-covered wall, they ignored me, hell bent on other pursuits.

On the seventh floor we found our client, together with her mother and grandmother. She was a frightened fifteen-year-old who looked about twelve. She had had no antenatal care and was completely unprepared for her baby. She had refused categorically to go into hospital, and her grandmother, whose flat it was, had said that she would deliver the baby! Considerable effort had been made by both the girl and her granny to hide the situation from the mother, who had learned of the pregnancy only the previous week and notified the local GP, who contacted us.

The mother was furious with her daughter, livid with her own mother and taciturn with us. The tense atmosphere compounded the girl's apprehension. Every time she had a contraction, she gasped with terror. We sent Granny into the sitting room and the mother into the kitchen to make tea, where we could hear her banging around and muttering to herself. We calmed our little client down, gave her some sedation, which made her sleepy and relaxed, and settled down for a long wait.

At about 6:00 a.m. she eventually produced a small 5 lb baby boy, who appeared healthy enough, despite his size. The girl's mother was in raptures of delight and she and Granny hugged each other, all antagonism forgotten. My midwife rolled her eyes.

Half an hour later, as we were about to leave, the girl began to bleed. Blood is like spilt milk: there always looks more of it than there actually is. But even so, the amount was alarming.

"Which neighbour has a phone?"

The client's mother, having only arrived on the scene a few days before, had no idea. My midwife dispatched me in search of one. "You'll have to bang on a few doors; there must be one in the block. Otherwise it's the tobacconist. They always open early."

I set off praying I wouldn't meet the dogs again. By the time I had found a phone and called an ambulance, everyone I had disturbed was out on the landing in dressing-gown and slippers, ready to be "helpful" as one elderly woman assured me. It was quite a feat manoeuvring a bleeding girl strapped to a chair down seven flights of stairs, even with the encouragement and advice of all the neighbours. I carried the bags, my midwife the baby.

"You'll have to go with her to the hospital," she said, handing the tiny bundle wrapped in towels over to me. "I've got the car and I'm certainly not leaving it here!"

She looked around at the wasteland surroundings, the unfinished potholed road, the abandoned furniture, the overturned bins, the absence of grass or trees or any play area for children, the towers themselves rising up out of the ground as if they had erupted brutally from the earth. Her lip curled in disgust. "Dear heavens, fancy having to bring up a child in this God-forsaken place!"

I could only agree with her. John Fitzgerald Kennedy Heights, along with many, many other towers, was demolished twenty or so years later, but not before they had damaged whole communities. They were a disastrous social experiment and the area has never recovered. When the towers came down, crowds gathered to watch and cheer.

Our young mother was discharged from hospital after a week, having refused all contraceptive advice and stating her intention to give up breastfeeding as soon as she could acquire baby milk and bottles. At least her mother's home was in a more respectable area. As Sister Hawkins said, "She's got her own front door, but I bet you we'll see her again next year."

CHAPTER 30

The "Leaving of Liverpool"

With the completion of my midwifery training, my uncertainty about my future became acute and I asked Mother Henrietta if I could make a retreat, to which she readily agreed. In the pleasant gardens of a nearby convent, I tried to put my thoughts in order and to think, not so much about what I wanted to do, but what I thought God wanted for me. Eventually I went to see the priest who was directing the retreat.

"There is so much about the religious life that I value. I have always loved community living; I have enormous affection and respect for my sisters, most of them anyway; I recognize the terrible, beautiful strength of the vows and I truly believe I have or had a vocation. I love God…"

"I hear a 'but' coming," he said, smiling sympathetically.

"It's just not enough for me any more. I want to do more, in both my professional and my personal life. I want to choose my friends, go where I want, read what I like, so I am resentful about the limitations that the life imposes. My vows, which once I felt so liberating, I now feel as a constraint. I know that I should be willing to submit to whatever is asked of me, and I know what Our Lord said about putting your hand to the plough and not looking back, but I am beginning to feel as if I'm ploughing the wrong furrow and furthermore that I'm even in the wrong field. Is this, as my Superior believes, just temptation? Will it pass?"

"It might, but you would have to regain what you've lost."

"What have I lost?" I asked unhappily.

"You've lost your religious spirit. The spirit you have at the moment may well be very good, but it's not the religious spirit. It's not the mindset that allows you to be at peace in your current situation."

Lost the religious spirit. It was the saddest phrase I had ever heard. It sounded so definitive.

"Could I get it back?" I was close to tears.

"Possibly, probably…" he paused, "if you wanted to. But you might have to go back a long way. It would be a hard journey and mean a complete re-evaluation of your life at the moment. I imagine you have been drifting away from it a long time."

In the following days I thought about my life since leaving the Noviciate. In retrospect, St Julien began to seem a sort of lovely pause; there was an unreality about my stay there. It was provisional; I was just marking time till I took on the reality of the religious life, which I came face to face with in Romiley. It occurred to me, I think for the first time, that the unhappy outcome of my time there had been my own doing. If I had been more obedient in spirit, more ready to submit, more humble, more conciliating, more nun-like, if I had prayed more, I might have saved myself and others a good deal of unhappiness.

I was fortunate in Mary-Mount, where I had found great happiness in the company of the sisters. But because I was out of the community most of the time, those other aspects of the life that *were* a problem for me weren't quickly identified, by myself or by Mother Henrietta. Instead, they were masked by my absence and by my enjoyment of what I was doing elsewhere. I didn't have the day-to-day irritations and compromises that a nun living out her life in a very restricted situation experiences and which might have tested me sooner.

After my retreat, Mother Henrietta asked me to take care of an elderly resident who was dying and who needed twenty-four-hour nursing. When I was able to join the community for Mass or the Office or meditation these activities took on great sweetness, because I began to believe that I had only a limited time left to share them. Sister Bernie, bringing me up a cup of tea or coffee, would pat my shoulder and look at me, her eyes and little snub nose crinkled in sadness.

"I'm praying for you all the time," she said.

Eventually I knew that I couldn't put it off any longer, so one morning, having asked to see her, on my knees I asked Mother Henrietta to apply to the bishop for a dispensation from my vows. She looked at me with deep sadness.

"Could you not wait," she asked, "until your vows expire? It's barely eighteen months away; you could leave then with no dispensation needed and you never know," she added brightly, "you might change your mind in the interim."

"I won't change my mind, Mother, and how can I stay, feeling as I do? If I put on a brave face, carry on as usual, the community will hope against hope that I might stay. If they see my unhappiness, it will make life wretched for them. If it were just a couple of months, maybe, but eighteen... it's too long."

"Have you been so unhappy?" she said miserably.

"I haven't been unhappy at all. Actually I've been very happy here. But I'm in the wrong place and it makes me uneasy and restless."

"When do you want to go?"

"As soon as it can be arranged."

"All right," she said heavily. "I'll send for the papers."

That afternoon Sister Superior drove me down into the city to buy suitable clothes. In the car park she broke down.

"Pull yourself together; I won't be able to go through with this if you don't help me. I'm relying on you," I said. Her distress was unexpected and disconcerted me.

"My green years were with you. How can you go and leave us? Oh, come on, let's get it over with."

In Lewis department store I bought a smart grey herringbone suit, and Sister Superior, having pulled herself together more or less, found me a pretty green blouse. Embarrassed, I told the shop assistant that I was going on a field trip. She looked astonished, as well she might.

"Wouldn't you do better with trousers and a warm jumper, Sister? They've got lovely anoraks in sportswear."

The ridiculousness of the situation made us both begin to giggle and the shop assistant got very sniffy, saying she was only trying to help. I needed shoes and tights, fortunately in a different department, so I didn't have to face the shop assistant again and explain why flesh-coloured tights and black patent leather court shoes were de rigueur for field trips that year!

Two days later the papers for my dispensation arrived and I signed them almost with relief. Mother Henrietta announced her intention of hanging on to them. She still believed that the Holy Spirit might bring me to my senses, and of course she could have been right.

"I'm going to keep your papers for a fortnight. Until they are registered you are still part of the congregation – you are on holiday if you like; compassionate leave; a field trip!"

Sister Teresa brought us in some coffee. She found it very difficult to say anything to me. Traditionally, nuns who were leaving slipped away quietly, often at night and with no ceremony or farewells. I knew that my imminent and open departure was hard for the community to handle and she was only uncertain about what she ought to say. We had got on very well together. When unexpectedly Bijou shuffled up to me and put his head on my knee, she burst out laughing.

"You see," said Mother Henrietta delightedly, "even Bijou wants you to stay."

A most extraordinary event occurred the evening before my departure. Taking pity on my anguish, Mother Henrietta sent me in the car to accompany her sister, who had been staying at Mary-Mount, home to her house on the Wirral. We needed to pick up keys from the neighbour. He settled us down while he went to fetch a sherry and, in his absence, I saw some framed engineering certificates on the wall, one relating to a power station in Dunoon, my birthplace. Delighted at my comments, he produced a photograph of a group of people standing in front of what he said was at that time a very modern piece of equipment. Behind him in the picture was a pretty, dark-haired girl. "That's Maisie McCutchion," I said.

"How on earth do you know?" he asked in astonishment.

"Because the girl in your photo is my mother!" I replied, smiling at him.

We stared at each other in amazement. It was the most astonishing coincidence of my life. It certainly momentarily distracted me that evening.

That night, back at Mary-Mount, I lay in bed looking at my habit hanging on the door and the grey suit beside it. So much flooded through my mind that I was sure I wouldn't sleep. I thought a great deal about the Noviciate and specifically about Sister Mistress of Novices and Sister Marie-Suzanne. I wished I had written to them. I pretended to myself that what had prevented me was the knowledge that permission would not have been given, but I knew that had I wanted to write, I would have done it anyway. It was shame that prevented me and an almost childish feeling that I was letting them down. In my reflections that night there was terrible sadness but also a certain elation and even excitement struggling to the surface. At about 11:00 p.m. I heard a knock. It was Sister Caroline.

"I know it's Great Silence but I had to say goodbye." She was in tears. Two others, Sister Lucinda and Sister Elizabeth, turned up before I eventually and surprisingly fell deeply asleep.

I was in the chapel for Laudes and Mass, although Mother Henrietta had told me to have a lie-in. She was not at breakfast. We ate as usual in silence: Sister Superior, pale as ash, ate nothing.

My train was at lunchtime so I helped calmly with the washing-up then went out into the garden to say my rosary; it seemed the sensible thing to do.

Mother Henrietta and Sister Superior called me in and, in the bright little parlour that I knew so well, I unpinned and took off my veil, kissing it automatically before untying my bandeau and laying it down. The memory of putting it on for the first time all those years ago slipped into my mind and I felt raw pain in my throat.

"Thank God we don't shave our heads like some nuns," said Sister Superior, "or we'd have had to buy a wig." She managed a smile. I had washed my hair the night before and it hung, thick and unfamiliar, curling on my shoulders. I stepped out of my habit and put on the pretty green blouse chosen for me and the neat grey suit.

"You look very nice," Mother Henrietta said encouragingly, and I smiled at her kindness, and thought with gratitude how sensible and practical she could be. I felt a pang when in answer to my request she said regretfully, "I'm sorry. You can't keep the crucifix."

With real regret and some resentment I surrendered the cross that I had worn on my breast for so many years. I couldn't think what possible reason there was for refusing it to me. I did keep my Office Book, and my Bible, together with several other books and all the sweet and loving holy pictures I had been sent the previous weeks.

My dowry of £30 was returned to me. When I looked at it, I saw I had been given twice that much. Mother Henrietta was insistent that if I found myself in need, I should let her know. Ever practical, she added, "Until you get a job, of course, not forever and ever."

My departure was brightened by the unexpected and determined arrival of several members of the community. Their affectionate support smoothed the moment of separation.

"I should have taken that skirt up." The sister who had made all my nurse's dresses for me looked regretfully at it. "It's a bit long for today's fashion." She was right, it was a little too long for the modern young woman I was about to become, but sartorial considerations had been the last thing on my mind in the previous few days.

"You've got good qualifications," interjected Sister Bernie. "You should be able to get a decent job. Just as long as you don't become a priest's housekeeper," she added brightly. She looked outraged at the burst of uneasy laughter that greeted this remark. "It's true," she retorted indignantly. "It's what a lot of ex-nuns do." She patted my cheek affectionately. "We'd feel let down; we've done better for you than that!"

At Lime Street station, Sister Superior went off to buy my ticket and we stood, Mother Henrietta and I, in a sort of tense silence. There wasn't anything left to say.

"Don't wait, Mother. I'll be fine."

"Of course we'll wait!"

I began to feel terribly tired, as if I had a great weight on my chest, and found it difficult to catch my breath. Then to my horror I began to cry aloud. It was not the quiet discreet tears that people often let fall at times of separation but great heaving, gulping, hysterical, and, above all, very noisy sobs. I thought of all the occasions I had said goodbye to nuns at railway stations and how I had always cried.

Poor Mother Henrietta and Sister Superior, who arrived back at my side with my ticket, looked not unreasonably both embarrassed and appalled. We were the object of considerable interest. Grasping my arm firmly, Mother Henrietta marched me into the bar and ordered me a brandy, telling the barman it was for health reasons, as I was unwell.

"Drink it up," she said firmly. It made me gasp but it stopped the noise. "Goodness, I didn't expect that, but then you always were unexpected." She smiled grimly at me.

I began to say sorry; sorry for going, for letting her down, for not living up to her expectations, for my bad behaviour in Romiley, for preferring my career to the religious life; sorry for anything I could think of. It seemed terribly important to say it all, the time was so short. She put a hand up to stop me, and repeated that nothing was as yet irrevocable. Sister Superior kissed me briefly at the barrier and turned away. Considering her distaste for human contact, I saw this as a deep expression of her affection. I watched her walk away, her lean elegant silhouette so familiar. I longed for her to turn around and wave but she didn't.

Mother Henrietta walked me down the platform to the train bound for the family home town of Portsmouth, and found me a seat. Putting her hands on my shoulders, she gave me a robust kiss on each cheek and then, indifferent to anybody overhearing, she said staunchly, "Listen to me. You can be very fascinating when you want." She laughed briefly. "You fascinate me and *I'm* a nun, so be careful! I know that you want to have children, and God willing so you will, but take the well-meant advice of an old woman and get the husband first; it's so much *neater*! Phone me, phone me!"

I laughed tearfully. The train began to pull away and her face slid back. Exhausted, I sank back onto the seat and discovered, after groping in my new handbag, that I had neither hanky nor tissue.

"Here." A kind hand proffered the latter. I took it gratefully and smiled my thanks to a girl about my own age, sitting across the carriage. She looked sympathetically at my tear-stained face.

"Do you want one of these? You look as if you could do with one."

I looked down at the packet of cigarettes tendered toward me.

"No, thank you," I said very seriously. "I'm trying to give it up, but it'll not be all that easy, kicking the habit."

Glossary

Bandeau, bonnet, or coif and veil: The headdress worn by nuns. The bandeau, bonnet, or coif is the white cap that covers the forehead, head and sometimes the shoulders. It is covered by a veil, usually white for the novices and black for the professed nuns.

Chapter of Faults: This is a practice common to almost all congregations, where the members meet at specified times to admit aloud, to their community, faults they may have committed against the Rule.

Congregation: A group of convents usually dedicated to the Virgin Mary or a particular saint, and governed by an elected General Superior, known as Reverend Mother General, and her councillors. The world's Roman Catholic nuns can be thought of as being like an immense army. This "army" is divided into various "congregations" or "orders", almost like "regiments". They have their own name, particular style, costume (the "habit"), way of life, and follow a set of rules known as the "Constitutions" or "Holy Rule", which are specific to each congregation. The congregation of the Sisters Of Charity of Our Lady of Evron comprised all those nuns in France, Canada, England, Ireland, Wales and Africa, including the postulants and novices living "under the flag" of that name.

A congregation may be large and international, or relatively small and regional. It can also be either a "Roman" congregation whose constitutions have been approved by the Vatican, or a "Diocesan" congregation under the direct control of the local bishop. The advantage of the former is that it is not subject to the possible arbitrary interference of the local bishop. The advantage of the latter is that any issues can be resolved swiftly at local level. The disadvantage of being a "Roman" congregation is that the Vatican is slow in its decision making process. The disadvantage of a "Diocesan" congregation is that the bishop has the right to intervene directly in the congregations internal affairs.

Convent: A building lived in by nuns and governed by a Sister Superior or Mother Superior.

General Chapter: This is a meeting held every few years, as specified in the Rule, to elect a Superior General and her Council, and to discuss and modify any administrative matter or change any aspect of the Rule (which must be ratified in Rome). A Superior General can only remain in her post for a specified time. Under some circumstances it is possible to re-elect her. The Superior General is elected by delegates who are themselves elected by the convent communities. Sometimes an extraordinary General Chapter is convoked for other reasons – the death in office of the Superior General, for example, or in response to an imperative demand from Rome, as was the case after the Second Vatican Council.

Gregorian plainchant: This is a music style that dates from the middle ages. For centuries it was the official music of the church. It is sung in Latin, with the words being taken from various books of the Bible. The chant is unaccompanied by any instrument. It is usually only sung nowadays by members of religious communities as part of their religious services and communal prayer.

Guardian angel: An angel allocated to take care of and protect an individual. Belief in guardian angels can be dated to the first centuries of Christianity. Belief in angels is part of the Roman Catholic tradition but there is no dogma attached to their existence and you do not have to believe in them.

Habit: The costume or uniform worn by nuns and monks, still an integral part of some communities but much less common today.

Mother House: This is normally the main convent of a congregation, and the administrative centre. The Superior General and her Council live there.

Novice: A woman accepted into a congregation or order who spends a specified time (usually one to two years) determined by the Constitutions studying and learning about the congregation, its works, its place in the Catholic Church, and its life of prayer, with a view to entering fully into it by means of the vows. She is not a religious but lives as if she is and is subject to all the obligations of the Holy Rule. She is free to leave at any time and can also be sent away if it is appropriate.

Noviciate: This is both the convent building that houses the novices and the period of time a novice spends training to become a nun. For the purposes of this book, a capital "N" is used to designate the building and a lower case "n" for the period of time. In some literature, "noviciate" is an alternative name for novice.

Nuns: Women who have taken vows, usually of poverty, chastity, and obedience, and who live in community, sharing a particular lifestyle as specified in their rules, which are called Constitutions.

An **Order:** This term is applied to the large monastic associations mainly: the Dominicans; the Benedictines; the Carthusians; the Cistercians, the Carmelites and the Franciscans. These associations, both male and female are largely contemplatives meaning their life is essentially one of manual work and prayer. They are all "Roman", answerable only to the Vatican.

Postulancy: A period of time specified by the Constitutions before the postulant is admitted to the congregation as a novice.

Postulant: A person who enters a Noviciate with the desire to become a novice and ultimately a nun. She does not wear the habit but usually some modified form of religious dress that identifies her status.

Province: If a congregation is sufficiently large, it will be broken down into provinces for ease of government. This is particularly so if the congregation is widely dispersed and/or international. Each province will be governed by a Sister Superior, known as Mother Provincial, and three councillors, all appointed by the Reverend Mother General and her councillors after consulting all the nuns of the province who have taken final vows.

Provincial Superior: She is usually given the title "Mother". With her councillors, she is answerable to the Superior General and her councillors. She is the Superior General's representative in the province.

A **religious:** Someone who is living the religious life.

The **religious life:** This is the life lived by men and women in convents, monasteries, etc., once they have taken their vows.

Religious profession: The taking of vows. When a novice makes her vows for a specified period of time she is bound by them until their expiry date. If she wishes to leave the congregation during this time, she must apply for a dispensation. Vows are usually taken annually over several years, as specified by the Constitutions. If a religious has made final or perpetual vows, which imply a permanent lifetime dedication, she has the right to remain, in sickness or in health, until the end of her life, and can only be dismissed for grave scandal. If a religious of a Roman congregation, having taken final vows, wishes to leave, dispensation must be granted by Rome. The local bishop alone cannot grant it. He will be informed and it may be that he, on behalf of the congregation, requests the dispensation. No person can be constrained in a congregation or order against their will. The vows are a commitment made to God within the framework of a religious institution and have no legal implication.

Rule or Holy Rule: This consists of the Constitutions and the written Customs and Practices of a congregation or order. The Constitutions are imperatives, and the Customs and Practices are guidelines.

Sister Superior: Appointed by the Superior General, she is responsible for the spiritual and material wellbeing of her community and is answerable first to the Mother Provincial and then to the Superior General. She must be a nun who has taken final vows. Her term of office is decided by the Constitutions, usually a period of three years. This term can be extended twice, and then there must be a hiatus of six months before she is reappointed to the same convent.

Superior General: She is usually titled Reverend Mother General or Reverend Mother. She must be a nun who has made her final vows and is elected by delegates in the course of a General Chapter. She is responsible for maintaining the spirit of the congregation and for supervising its efficient functioning in every way. Among other duties, the Superior General and her councillors appoint the **Provincial Superior** and the **Sister Superior** for each convent in the congregation.

St Jude: Patron saint of hopeless cases and lost things.